# This Is Ballroom Dance

### Lois Ellfeldt

Professor Emeritus, University of Southern California

GV
1751
.E42
1974

Ellfeldt, Lois.                             78756
    This is ballroom dance / by Lois
Ellfeldt, Virgil L. Morton. Illustrated
by Hilda Sachs. 1st ed. Palo Alto,
Calif.: National Press Books, c1974.
    vi, 114 p. : ill. ; 23 cm. (National
Press Books dance activities series)
    Bibliography: p. 110-111.
    ISBN 0-87484-245-X


    1. Ballroom dancing.   I. Morton,
Virgil L., joint author.   II. Title

03 JUL 85        814672   OMMMxc        73-84770

GV
1751
.E42
1974

Library of Congress Catalog Card Number: 73-84770
International Standard Book Numbers:   0-87484-244-1  (paper)
                                       0-87484-245-X (cloth)

Manufactured in the United States of America

National Press Books, 850 Hansen Way, Palo Alto, California 94304

This book was set in Aldine Roman Medium by Libra Cold Type and printed by Kingsport
Press. The designer was Nancy Sears. Sponsoring editor was Richard W. Bare, project
editor was Zipporah Collins, and Michelle Hogan supervised production.

# Contents

# Preface

Popular music and ballroom dance bear the sharp imprint of time. Each stands as a symbol of its period. Both are ever changing, yet strangely the same, even as people are ever changing, yet the same. In spite of differences in step pattern, musical accompaniment, dynamics, style, and relationship between the dancers, certain principles and movement patterns persist, untouched by successive generations. If a book on ballroom dance is to have more than temporary value, it must be concerned with these basic principles and movement patterns

This book presents some of the fundamentals that should prove helpful to both student and teacher. Common elements among dance forms are pointed out, and differences are identified only to clarify unique characteristics. For example, the fox trot, waltz, and tango box steps are all performed in the same way, although the rhythm, dynamics, and style may change. The difference between a double lindy in swing, a two-step in the samba, and the pony in rock is not in their step pattern but rather in the size of the step, where it is done, and the relationship of the partners.

Ballroom dance affords the opportunity for young men and women to work together in a physical activity that is pleasant and beneficial for both. Physical benefits include the rhythmic exercise of the entire muscular structure, coordination of mind and muscles, relaxation, and the development of endurance, vigor, flexibility, and habits of proper posture. Social benefits include the experience of learning to cooperate with and become more tolerant of other people. Frequently a shy person will blossom forth with self-confidence and more mature stability, while an extrovert may learn to channel his talents more creatively. The many varieties of music used in ballroom dance will broaden the dancer's outlook and knowledge of the entire musical field.

The terms *ballroom dance, social dance,* and *salon dance* are all applied to popular dancing—the many couple dances that have become a part of the American heritage—done in public or private ballrooms, at church socials, in school gymnasiums, or wherever else people meet to enjoy it. All terms may be used interchangeably. *Rock dance* and *discotheque dance* are terms applied to those special dances inspired by rock 'n' roll music; they too are an important facet of the vast field of American ballroom dance.

The dance descriptions presented here are arranged historically, in the order in which they became a part of the American dance scene. This does not mean they should necessarily be taught in that order. Each group of students will vary, depending on their age, their former dance experience, the tastes of the community in which they reside, and other related circumstances, and the teacher should choose the order of dances that best fits the students. No book, no matter how skillfully written, can substitute for the skill and experience of a well-trained teacher.

## Key to Abbreviations

| | |
|---|---|
| bkwd | backward |
| CCW | counterclockwise |
| CW | clockwise |
| diag | diagonal(ly) |
| fwd | forward |
| LF | left foot |
| LOD | line of direction |
| meas | measure(s) |
| Q | quick |
| RF | right foot |
| S | slow |
| swd | sideward |
| wt | weight |

# 1

# This Is Ballroom Dance

The word *dance* is used to describe many kinds of unusual actions—the twinkling of stars, the twirling of a ballerina, seagulls skimming across a beach, or the snap-jerk-roll of hard rock. Elephants dance; so do atoms, snowflakes, and lightning across the sky. Ice-skating is dance on ice, swimming is dance in the water, and skydiving is dance in the air. Today we are faced with a variety of dance forms that are often difficult to tell apart. It is apparent that we need help in making the differentiations clear.

## DEFINITIONS

The unifying characteristic of all dance is movement—the action of people moving. But we also move in lawn tennis and a Veteran's Day parade. Indeed, movement is essential in everything people do, from birth to death. What then is unique to that movement called *dance*? Basically it is the fact that we *call* it dance. Certainly it is not unique because it is rhythmic, for there is little movement that is not rhythmic. Nor is it unique because it is accompanied by music, for much dance has nothing to do with music.

Aside from a loose use of the term to describe some exotic action, *dance* is used to refer to human movement designed to fulfill some nonfunctional purpose, stated or not. Sometimes dance serves to entertain or to provide a spectacle for an audience: it may animate colorful staging or costume effects, it may exhibit physical virtuosity, it may provide erotic stimulation, or it may display a well-proportioned body or a glamourous personality. Some kinds of dance provide an avenue for therapy. Dance may exist as a performing art or a means of celebrating national, ethnic, or group relationships. Or it may frankly fulfill an urge to play, to socialize, to have fun.

What is the purpose of *ballroom dance*? In spite of periodic changes in its form and style, ballroom dance remains *a socially acceptable celebration of the relationship of boys and girls, men and women, in a recreational framework.* While display, entertainment of others, and technical skill may be emphasized by many dancers, *participation* is more important than *performance*. Regardless of their spatial relationship as partners, it is male-female participation within a group structure that is the essence of ballroom dance. Socialization, play, and fun are its basic elements. The extent to which any social dance reflects earlier coming-of-age ceremonies, fertility rites, or courtship rituals can only be surmised.

## BRIEF HISTORY AND DEVELOPMENT

In primitive societies, dance was an important part of most magic ceremonies for assuring food, power, and survival—life itself. This was "social dance" in the broadest sense, celebrating birth, membership in the group, marriage, death, success in the hunt, other social occasions, and plain fun. There is little doubt that these dances were forerunners of our social dances, but the point of view and purpose of dancers are quite different today. From a profound belief in the magical properties of the ritual we have turned to a relatively superficial male-female performance of movement in the manner of the time. Nevertheless, current dancers sometimes seem to attain a kind of contemporary belief in the magical properties of the ritual.

It is hard to say whether there has been conscious use of the movements from ancient rituals through the years. But because men move in much the same ways, regardless of time and place, there is probably less variation than we might at first imagine. However, there is no doubt that changes have occurred in the purpose, the relationships of dancers to each other, the tempo and rhythm in which they move, the dynamics of their actions, and, most particularly, that illusive element called *style*.

Variations in ballroom dance do not appear at random. They reflect the current social order and particularly relationships among people: social attitudes about women, the role of men, social customs, and ideologies. Over a period of time some dances disappear, and others take their place. Some dances last for a long time, others are gone overnight, and some reappear in other guises.

It is difficult to identify basic differences between folk dance and ballroom dance today. When it started, folk dance, like primitive ceremonial dances, was steeped in magic. In time, however, the dances came to be a commemoration of the original purposes, which dealt with the work patterns, traditions, and national flavor of a people. There are intermittent revivals of "authentic folk dances" in which the participants seek to recapture original forms, feelings, and styles. Seldom is it possible to do so completely, for time and place have changed, and the dance is simply a rehearsal of a tradition. The value of revivals lies in presenting a period piece, an attempt at living history. Today most folk dances, like ballroom dances, are done for their socializing and recreational value.

According to most historical records it was in thirteenth-century Provence, in southern France, that the rustic line and circle dance done by peasants evolved into the forerunner of our ballroom dance. Not coincidental was development of the theme of romantic love and knightly regard for pure maidens who personified the Holy Virgin. A new relationship of man to woman and new patterns for Western etiquette were established. When the line dances done outdoors in fields moved into the confining rooms of the nobles, their formations and figures had to change. Turns, bows, and interchanges of partners replaced line formations that could be done by a group of dancers all holding each others' hands.

It has been said that ballroom dance developed out of the desire of the aristocracy to display their costumes, manners, and elaborate deportment while still participating in a pleasurable activity. Apparently dance was an ideal medium for exalting personalities, manners, and class. Taking the dances at hand—the bawdy dances of the rustics and the solemn church processionals—aristocrats embellished them for great court balls and royal entertainment.

During this period there was a distinct difference between the dance of common people and the dance of nobles. While both might do the same steps, the aristocrats moved solemnly with precision and dignity, while the peasants leaped and stomped their feet, shouting and whirling in dizzy circles. At court, the mark of true gentlemen and ladies was their skill and grace in dance, their ability to move in the precise patterns. During the sixteenth century, the stately basse dance and pavane were popular. Soon dancing masters assumed the responsibility for teaching new dances (and acceptable behavior and manners) to members of the court. Popular dances of the time included the courante, gavotte, saraband, minuet, gigue, and bourrée, and music was written especially for them. These preclassic music forms are still played, but most of the dances have been long forgotten.

By the nineteenth century, as the class structure began to break down, there was increasing similarity in the dances of all people in the Western world. Many went to the popular dance halls, and uniformity in both form and style of dance participation was fostered. The major distinction that remained was in *where* the dances took place. The final protection for the "aristocracy" was provided by the private party or the exclusive assembly hall. The presentation ball of today's debutante is probably the current version. A pastime available to the masses apparently loses something of its social prestige.

The close relationship between social history and dance history can be illustrated in many ways. The estampie and carole, rustic peasant dances, were introduced into the royal courts of Europe by courtiers and troubadors who fled

Provence after the Albigensian massacre. Dances associated with the intrigues and alliances of the Italian courts were introduced by Catherine de Médicis to the courts of France. After the Polish revolution of 1831 there was widespread acceptance of the polka and the polonaise as popular ballroom dances the world around. The continuing influence of black people on the music and dance of North and South America has been apparent from the time of Negro slave songs and dances, through blues, jazz, and swing to rock. The rise of no-contact, individual yet group-structured rock dances of the late sixties and early seventies reflects another view of contemporary life.

Consider the stately bows and sober processions of the sixteenth-century court dances; the mincing steps of the seventeenth-century minuet; the striding walk of the turn of the century one-step and fox trot; the persistent broken rhythm of the World War II jitterbug and swing; the rotating twist of the sixties; and the jagged rock contortions of the seventies. Each of these might well serve as a stereotype of its time.

The changing relationship between men and women has had considerable influence on ballroom dance. The medieval concept of chivalrous love resulted in a constrained and delicate dance of knights and ladies. The accent on manners, convention, and costume clearly affected the elegant and artificial French court dance. With the emancipation of women came waltzes, polkas, and other closed-couple dances in which women were permitted—even encouraged—to dance with many different partners. Jitterbug appeared as a casual and relatively crude performance by boy and girl in a far less idealized relationship. The trend to unisex styles, indiscriminate leadership roles, and no-contact rock dance all suggest another kind of boy-girl relationship.

Today's discotheque provides an opportunity for individually chosen and performed dance. Here, a kind of "freedom" is available to all, regardless of training or background. But let it not be said that there are no traditional steps or no tightly structured group setting. It is simply a different kind of uniformity that is being sponsored. And, with worldwide communication through television, radio, and nearly instant travel, dance is more and more alike around the globe. We in the United States may assume that current dance forms are ours, but young people in Tokyo, Helsinki, Athens, Buenos Aires, Capetown, and Addis Ababa are probably doing the same dances. More and more it is really one world in dance.

# 2

# Elements of Ballroom Dancing

There are two distinct classes of ballroom dance, according to the positions used by the male and female partners. In the older, traditional, dance form, the man holds and leads the woman in a body-contact position while progressing counterclockwise around the dancing area. In the more contemporary forms, usually performed to rock music, separated couples face each other and move according to their own interpretations of the musical rhythm.

In the contact-partnered dance, the man leads his partner into certain combinations of steps suitable to the music. These combinations are usually composed of progression steps, turning figures, and steps remaining in one place. In the no-contact dance, the dancers seldom travel but rather are limited to movements in one place. Since there is rarely any physical contact in this type of dance, each partner is free to improvise and embellish his own action. While many figures have become associated with specific dances of this category, the movements are basically nonlocomotor, freely using rotating, stretching, and swinging combinations of the pelvis, trunk, shoulders, head, and arms.

While the no-contact dances are especially popular with younger dancers, there are many people, young and old, who also enjoy the traditional partnered dances, such as the fox trot, the cha-cha, the tango, and the waltz. Both forms have many elements in common. Developing a sensitivity to rhythm, patterning, and style will greatly enhance and improve a dancer's ability to do all forms of dance.

## BALLROOM DANCE RHYTHMS

Ballroom dance should be performed to music played by an orchestra that specializes in this type of music. A good dance orchestra will emphasize the *underlying beat* of the music. A good dancer must be able to hear and respond to this beat. The beat is what enables the dancer to distinguish a waltz from a fox trot, a rumba, or whatever else the piece may be. The dancer must not try to discover the dance rhythm from the *name* of the musical selection. A good musical arranger can take any melody and turn it into a waltz, samba, fox trot, or any other dance.

In American ballroom dance, the most common rhythm is *duple* meter. This means that the music is constructed rhythmically with *two* dominant beats, or some multiple of two beats, to the musical measure. The musical signature may be either 2/4 time or 4/4 time. Both time signatures, however, should produce a clear two-beat rhythm. In 2/4 time, the count of 1 is usually stressed, producing a count of *1-2/ 1-2/* etc. In 4/4 time, counts 1 and 3 are usually stressed, producing a pattern of *1-2-3-4/ 1-2-3-4/* etc.

The differences between the 2/4 and 4/4 time signatures are frequently so subtle that only an experienced musician can distinguish them by ear. But beginning dancers should be able to distinguish both forms of the two-beat rhythm from other time signatures after only a short experience in listening.

Although most American ballroom dances use either 2/4 or 4/4 time, each dance employs the rhythm in a characteristic manner, marking it as a samba, a tango, a cha-cha, or some other dance. These distinguishing characteristics will be further identified at the discussions of each dance.

The 2/4 meter indicates that there are two quarter notes, or the equivalent, in each musical measure, and it is written:

The 4/4 meter indicates that there are four quarter notes, or the equivalent, in each measure, and it is written:

The accent marks indicate the stresses usually found in these two rhythms, but there are numerous variations from one dance to another.

The only other time signature used in American ballroom dances is 3/4 meter. In past centuries, many of the court dances of France, Italy, Spain, and England were composed in 3/4 meter. These included the polonaise, galliard, courante, sevillanas, Spanish bolero, and saraband. At the beginning of the twentieth century, the popular dances in this meter included the varsoviana, three-step, mazurka, veleta, and redowa. Currently, the only dance using the 3/4 marking is the American waltz, a slower and technically less difficult version of the Viennese waltz which dominated the popular dance field throughout the nineteenth century.

The 3/4 meter, also known as *triple* meter, has three beats to a measure, each having the value of a quarter note. It is written:

In all waltzes, the first note in each measure is accented. The beginning dancer needs to recognize the accented note as the count of 1, because there is a specific foot movement for each count of the waltz.

## Better Rhythmic Perception

Since dance movement usually follows or augments the musical rhythm, it is imperative that dancers recognize rhythm patterns. Current dance music is mostly in duple and occasionally in triple meter. The underlying beat is usually clear, and the pattern obvious. But some people find it difficult to differentiate musical rhythms. Some can hear the rhythm but are unable to move with it. Some neither hear nor are consciously aware of any pattern. There is no simple solution to these problems, but we can offer some suggestions that have worked for some students.

One difficulty experienced in follower-leader partnered dances is entirely psychological. The boy finds his responsibilities for leading, making decisions, and being so close to a girl overwhelming. Rhythmic perception is the least of his concerns, and he pays no attention to music, dance position, leading, or what he is doing. His problem is not that he cannot identify rhythm, but rather that his attitude to the entire situation blocks all his senses. With some girls, acceptance of the role of follower as well as the proximity of a boy may cause similar or other unexpected difficulties. These reactions do not mean that the dancers lack a sense of rhythm!

Solutions to such personality problems are not offered here, but we do suggest the following for improving rhythmic acuity in dancers who lack it.

1. Listen to social dance music in both 4/4 and 3/4 meters. Clap on the first beat of each measure.

    1        2        3        4
    clap

    1        2        3
    clap

Clap on each beat of a 4/4 measure and a 3/4 measure.

| 1 | 2 | 3 | 4 |
|:---:|:---:|:---:|:---:|
| clap | clap | clap | clap |

| 1 | 2 | 3 |
|:---:|:---:|:---:|
| clap | clap | clap |

2. Listen to a 4/4 underlying beat and clap each beat of the four, accenting count 1 of each measure. Then try to clap a pattern of three, accenting count 1 of each measure, to the same music. Usually the accents that do not coincide with the music are easily heard. Trying to clap a pattern of four while listening to a 3/4 meter is equally difficult.

3. Clap alternate beats of a 4/4 rhythm.

| 1 | 2 | 3 | 4 |
|:---:|:---:|:---:|:---:|
| clap | | clap | |

Now clap twice as fast on the beats that had no clap before (*held* beats).

| 1 | 2 | 3 | 4 |
|:---:|:---:|:---:|:---:|
| clap | clap-clap | clap | clap-clap |

4. Walk to a 4/4 rhythm, stepping on alternate beats.

| 1 | 2 | 3 | 4 |
|:---:|:---:|:---:|:---:|
| step | | step | |

Clap on the alternate beats that had no step before.

| 1 | 2 | 3 | 4 |
|:---:|:---:|:---:|:---:|
| | clap | | clap |

5. Combine the walk and the clap.

| 1 | 2 | 3 | 4 |
|:---:|:---:|:---:|:---:|
| step | clap | step | clap |

6. Reverse the action so that you now step where before you clapped and vice versa.

| 1 | 2 | 3 | 4 |
|:---:|:---:|:---:|:---:|
| clap | step | clap | step |

7. Step on each beat of the measure.

| 1 | 2 | 3 | 4 |
|:---:|:---:|:---:|:---:|
| step | step | step | step |

Now step twice as slowly.

| 1 | 2 | 3 | 4 |
|---|---|---|---|
| step | | step | |

Now step twice as fast as the first time.

| 1 | 2 | 3 | 4 |
|---|---|---|---|
| step-step | step-step | step-step | step-step |

8. Alternate slow and fast steps.

| 1 | 2 | 3 | 4 |
|---|---|---|---|
| step | step-step | step | step-step |

Do this simple combination.

| 1 | 2 | 3 | 4 |
|---|---|---|---|
| step | | step-step | step-step |

### Counting Rhythm Sequences

Dancers must not only learn to *hear* the music of various dances but also learn to *count* the rhythm. This is especially important for accomplishing figures that have changes of rhythms. Although a dancer need not count the rhythm in the same manner an experienced musician would, the count must be rhythmically equivalent.

The easiest, and probably the most frequently used, method of counting social dance rhythms is by "quicks" and "slows." Two quicks rhythmically are the equivalent of one slow. Each count represents a change of weight. Thus, a measure of music in 4/4 time in which two changes of weight are made on the second note may be counted by the following methods:

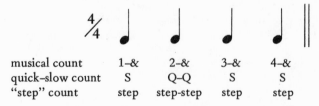

| | musical count | 1-& | 2-& | 3-& | 4-& |
|---|---|---|---|---|---|
| | quick-slow count | S | Q-Q | S | S |
| | "step" count | step | step-step | step | step |

It is important to remember that single notes can be divided into two quicks only in 2/4 or 4/4 music. In 3/4 rhythm each of the three notes is consistently of equal duration.

In most dances, the quicks are not written into the music. They are made at the discretion of the man leading the dance or according to certain patterns of the dance.

## SELECTING THE CORRECT MUSIC

The use of correctly played and accented music is vital to good ballroom dancing. Each dance has its own characteristic rhythm, which must be distinctly and easily heard by the dancers. Most music heard on radio and television is not generally suitable for dancing because it is designed for listening; that is, the melodic line is stressed while the underlying rhythmic beat is played more softly. Although all music has rhythmic structure, for the beginning dancer this structure must be definite enough to be distinguished readily. Even advanced dancers quickly lose interest if they have to strain to hear the beat.

A dance orchestra, as distinguished from a symphonic or other orchestra, will stress the base rhythm that the dancer uses to identify the particular dance and to follow.

Fortunately, several companies make a specialty of producing records for ballroom dance. They are authorities on dance rhythms and take pride in offering correctly played music for the ballroom dance field. A postcard request to any of the following firms will bring a catalog of their dance selections by return mail:

Dance Along Records, 111 West 57th Street, New York, N.Y. 10019.
Hoctor Records, P. O. Box 38, Waldwick, N.J. 07463.
Orion Records, 614 Davis Street, Evanston, Ill. 60201.
Twelgrenn, Inc., P. O. Box 16, Bath, Ohio 44210.
Roper Records, 48–16 43rd Avenue, Long Island City, N.Y. 11104.

For the more traditional dance forms, the old "standard" melodies are frequently the most satisfying to dancers, especially beginners.

In the area of rock 'n' roll music, young dancers like selections that are currently popular. As these tunes quickly drop out of favor, they have to be replaced frequently. Rock 'n' roll music is readily obtainable in most record shops and need not be ordered from specialty recording firms.

If recordings are to be kept for a long time the delicate microgrooves should be protected from scratches by wiping the records clean, keeping them in their original paper jackets, and placing them in albums where they will not rub together.

## BASIC DANCE STEPS

The remarkable similarity in the movements of all social dances is not always evident to a person observing good dancers. The steps of a cha-cha may appear to differ markedly from those of a fox trot; a tango from rock; a waltz from swing. But the differences lie in rhythm, sequence, relationship of dancers, and certain features characteristic of the dance, not in the steps being done.

## Moving through Space

With few exceptions, dancers move by transferring their weight from one foot to the other. This occurs in *walk, two-step,* and *pursuit* figures.

The *dance walk* is similar to ordinary walking but with a few refinements.

1. The leg swings straight forward or backward from the hip, with the knee and the ankle straightening into extension.
2. In most dances, the toe touches the floor first, whereas in a normal walk the heel touches the floor first.
3. The feet remain close to the floor, although they never drag; they either glide or pick up.
4. Generally, the feet remain under the body (with some exceptions as noted later in the instructions). The feet need to remain parallel to each other in passing from one step to another. Keeping the feet far apart produces an awkward "straddle" posture.
5. Step length is determined by the styling of each specific dance.
6. In fast-tempo dances, steps are relatively shorter than those taken with slower music.
7. As the weight transfers to the stepping foot, the knee should be relaxed to avoid jarring movements.
8. When turning, the dancer must pivot on the ball of the foot bearing the weight. To step flat on that foot would inhibit the turning action.

Variations on the dance walk are made by combining slow and quick walks. These changing rhythmic patterns are used in almost all ballroom dances.

The *two-step* is a combination of steps that progresses easily through space, either forward or backward, and lends itself to fast turns. (Because this figure involves three changes of weight, some dance authorities use the term *three-step* for the same combination.)

The following chart depicts the use of this step combination in various dances.

| Man | Two-step Counts | Fox trot Counts | Rock Counts | Woman |
|---|---|---|---|---|
| Step on LF | 1 | 1 | 1 | Step on RF |
| Close RF to LF & change wt | & | & | & | Close LF to RF & change wt |
| Step on LF | 2–& | 2–& | 2–& | Step on RF |
| Step on RF | 1 | 3 | 1 | Step on LF |
| Close LF to RF & change wt | & | & | & | Close RF to LF & change wt |
| Step on RF | 2–& | 4–& | 2–& | Step on LF |

The *pursuit*, or *travel*, figure is a combination of three changes of weight that is repeated in a series of alternating steps to move either forward or backward for as long as the dancers desire. It is similar to the two-step except that the second change of weight is made slightly to the side, rather than completely in line with the leading first step. The floor pattern is a *triangular*, or *half-square*, figure.

The following chart depicts use of the pursuit figure in three dances.

| Man | Waltz Counts | Fox trot Counts | Tango Counts | Woman |
|---|---|---|---|---|
| Step fwd on LF | 1 | 1–2 | 1 | Step bkwd on RF |
| Step fwd and to side on RF | 2 | 3 | & | Step fwd and to side on LF |
| Close LF to RF and change wt | 3 | 4 | 2–& | Close RF to LF and change wt |

To progress in either direction, the pursuit figure must alternate; that is, if the first measure begins with the left foot, the second measure will begin with the right foot, and so on.

## Moving Back and Forth

By alternating three changes of weight in place, a *balance* figure is formed. The following chart depicts the two-step in this variation.

| Man | Waltz Counts | Fox trot Counts | Rock Counts | Woman |
|---|---|---|---|---|
| Step on LF in place | 1 | 1 | 1 | Step on RF in place |
| Balance on RF and change wt | 2 | 2 | & | Balance on LF and change wt |
| Step on LF in place | 3 | 3–4 | 2–& | Step on RF in place |
| Step on RF in place | 1 | 1 | 1 | Step on LF in place |
| Balance on LF and change wt | 2 | 2 | & | Balance on RF and change wt |
| Step on RF in place | 3 | 3–4 | 2–& | Step on LF in place |

This combination of balance steps may be initiated either forward or backward or from side to side.

The *box* (also called a *square*) figure is common to many dances. It is so termed because the dancer's feet move in a square, or box formation on the floor. Actually, the figure consists of two triangular patterns, each triangle having three changes of weight. If the first triangle is initiated forward, the second one will lead backward, forming the completed square. Because of the reversal of movement, the box or square figure is made in place. The chart depicts boxes in various dances. It is also correct to initiate the box with the man leading backward and the woman stepping forward.

| Man | Waltz Counts | Fox trot Counts | Tango Counts | Woman |
|---|---|---|---|---|
| Step fwd on LF | 1 | 1–2 | 1–& | Step bkwd on RF |
| Step fwd & to side on RF | 2 | 3 | 2 | Step bkwd & to side on LF |
| Close LF to RF & change wt | 3 | 4 | & | Close RF to LF & change wt |

This forms the first triangle; to complete the square, the figure is reversed.

| | | | | |
|---|---|---|---|---|
| Step bkwd on RF | 1 | 1–2 | 3–& | Step fwd on LF |
| Step bkwd & to side on LF | 2 | 3 | 4 | Step fwd & to side on RF |
| Close RF to LF & change wt | 3 | 4 | & | Close LF to RF & change wt |

The *step-hold* is just that—an alternation of step and hold taken in opposite directions on opposite feet. Sometimes the hold, or second movement is done as a balance, a toe-touch, or even a swing of the free foot either forward or backward.

| Man | Waltz Counts | Fox trot Counts | Rock Counts | Woman |
|---|---|---|---|---|
| Step on LF | 1 | 1–2 | 1–& | Step on RF |
| Hold (or balance, swing, or tap) | 2–3 | 3–4 | 2–& | Hold (or balance, swing, or tap) |
| Step on RF | 1 | 1–2 | 1–& | Step on LF |
| Hold (or balance, swing, or tap) | 2–3 | 3–4 | 2–& | Hold (or balance, swing, or tap) |

The *slide* is made up of a continual "chase" of one foot after the other. Although usually done to the side, it may also move in other directions. Changing from one direction to another usually occurs after a one-beat hold, when the foot on the side of the new direction is free.

| Man | Waltz Counts | Fox trot Counts | Tango Counts | Woman |
|---|---|---|---|---|
| Step to side on LF | 1–2 | 1 | 1 | Step to side on RF |
| Chase with RF & change wt | 3 | 2 | & | Chase with LF & change wt |
| Step to side on LF | 1–2 | 3 | 2 | Step to side on RF |
| Chase with RF & change wt | 3 | 4 | & | Chase with LF & change wt |

### Remaining in Place (Nonlocomotor Movement)

The essence of rock dance is nonlocomotor movement. Rock dance is not *one* dance, but rather applies to a vast field of dances performed to rock 'n' roll music. The introduction of the twist in 1960 almost instantly opened a new era and style of ballroom dancing. Partners no longer adhered to traditional dance forms but freely improvised steps and movements in a no-contact position to the throbbing, pulsating two-beat rhythm of rock 'n' roll music.

Over more than a decade, rock has inspired a multitude of dances bearing different names. But all are based on vigorous movements of the torso, hips, and arms, and some use pantomimic actions.

In the majority of rock dances, each person remains in place facing a partner but each is free to create his or her own steps and body movements according to individual skill without any attempt to mirror the actions of the other. Although there are no set foot patterns, the examples given in the chapter are typical of those used by many dancers. Superimposed on a base of footwork, the action of the body introduces other accents. Together they may form complex movement patterns. In general, the body action consists of:

1. Body bends, shakes, and twists;
2. Head rolls, jerks, and "pecks;"
3. Double knee bends and straightenings;
4. Single knee bends with alternate foot balancing, tapping, or swinging;
5. Single or double hip swings, rolls, bumps, and grinds;
6. Arm and shoulder swings, jerks, and shakes.

Because the rock dancer has the chance to be truly creative he should explore all variations in direction, size, level, tempo, and duration of any simple body movement. Next, he should consider intensity, quality, and accent. These are the tools for discovering new and different movement patterns.

### DANCE POSITIONS

There are a number of variations on any position assumed for ballroom dance. In the traditional form, however, there are two basic relationships of the partners.

These are termed *closed dance position* and *open dance position*.

Closed dance position is also frequently termed *Ballroom position*, or *waltz position*. It is illustrated in figure 1.

*Figure 1*

1. The partners face each other, shoulders and hips parallel.

2. The man moves *slightly* to his left so that his feet are in position to step between those of his partner. This brings the partners into a position in which they are looking slightly over each other's right shoulders.

3. The man places his right arm around the woman's back, placing his hand approximately below her left shoulder blade. (His exact hand position will vary according to the height of his partner. The position must also change at times to facilitate leading various figures.) The man's right elbow is below his shoulder line and slightly away from his body.

4. The woman's left hand should be placed on the man's right shoulder. This will assist her in sensing his "body lead." Her left hand must *never* rest on the man's upper arm. (A rare exception may be made for an extremely short woman dancing with a very tall man.) No matter how delicate her hand may be, it can serve to throw the man off balance and hinder his leading by resting on his upper arm.

5. The man holds the woman's right hand in his left hand. The arms are slightly curved, elbows downward, with the clasped hands held at approximately the man's shoulder level. It is important for the woman to retain enough tension in her right arm to feel and respond to the lead given by the man's left hand. In general, the arms remain in this position in all closed-position dances; excessive arm movements are to be avoided.

6. The exact distance between partners will vary with each dance and with individual figures within a dance. Each partner, however, must maintain his balance in a manner comfortable to both dancers. Leaning on one's partner and embracing in a bear hug ceased to be good dancing form prior to World War I.

7. A good, but relaxed, posture should be maintained in the majority of closed-position dances. The body weight of each dancer should be brought forward to rest over the balls of the feet. Hips are kept from sagging backward by slightly lifting and controlling the abdominal muscles.

The *semi-open position,* also termed the *promenade position,* is between closed and open position (see figure 2).

*Figure 2*

1. From the closed dance position, the partners turn into a partly open position in which the man's right side and the woman's left side are together. The angle of the open position can vary from slight to full opening, with the partners facing in the same direction.

2. The arm positions shift slightly as the bodies turn, but they remain in the same relationship as in the closed position.

3. The man steps forward with his left foot, the woman with her right.

In the *open dance position,* the partners turn from the closed dance position into a fully open position, releasing their clasped hands (see figure 3). The man's right side and woman's left side are adjacent, with both partners facing the same direction. The inside arm positions may vary; the man may retain the arm hold behind the woman's back, or the dancers may join inside hands. They may also turn in place to bring their other hips and arms adjacent.

*Figure 3*

The *challenge position* (also termed the *no-contact position*) is used in dances where the individual performs alone. There is still a semblance of the traditional couple relationship in that the partners are opposite each other, just far enough apart so that they will not interfere with each other's movements (see figure 4). They usually focus attention on each other, but this varies with individual dancers. Because there is little progression through space, action occurs within the individual's own spatial area.

*Figure 4*

# 3

---

# *Leading and Following*

In a number of traditional ballroom dances with partners in body-contact position, the man assumes the role of leader. Since this is a cooperative affair, dancers must develop the ability to lead or follow. Experienced dancers are seldom conscious of either giving specific lead indications or reacting in a good following manner. Rather this has become a habitual part of their dance behavior.

## LEADING

The man, as the leader in a traditional dance, is responsible for determining the tempo, rhythm, and special characteristics of the music and then for choosing and directing the couple's movements. This involves telling the woman by strong and definite signals where, when, and how to move.

Self-assurance and calm, steady insistence on his chosen patterns are necessary to convince a partner that he is indeed leading. The male must *never* permit a female partner to take over and lead the dance.

Subtle indications of leading are given with body inclination and foot movement. A sensitive follower will immediately pick up both directional and dynamic cues.

As the leader moves forward, the momentum of his *body,* beginning with the chest, precedes his stepping foot. If the dance position is correct, and the woman is ready to be led, this motion will tell her to be ready to move backward.

Working in opposition to the feet, the *shoulders* indicate the position from which a step is to be done. They twist in the direction of a turn that is to be made, and, when the man plans to move to the side, the shoulder on that side is lowered.

The *right arm and hand* regulate speed and direction of movement. The man exerts a firm pressure for slow walks and a subsequent release of pressure for faster walks. He pulls his partner toward him to lead a walk backward, and pushes toward her when he walks forward. Pressure with the heel of his right hand and a shoulder twist to his left turns his partner into an open dance position. The *left hand* can exert a pull or push pressure that gives further directional cues.

Only when all these leads are combined can the man firmly and gently manipulate his partner's movements into the pattern chosen.

## Cues for Good Leading

1. Assume a good dance position.
2. Hold your partner firmly to give her confidence, but not so tightly as to restrict her movements.
3. Listen to the music. Correctly identify the rhythm, tempo, and accent, so that the steps you choose will fit.
4. Be sure you know the step before you try to lead it.
5. Keep your left foot free, and be ready to step out onto the ball of the foot, transferring your weight cleanly from one foot to the other.
6. Do not attempt complicated step patterns with a new partner.
7. Remember that a few simple steps done with precision and style are far better than intricate patterns poorly executed.
8. Establish the rhythmic pattern with a simple step in *closed position* and in *one place* before changing to open position, or moving through space or in turns.
9. Time each lead indication so that you give it *before* a change is to be done. This gives your partner an opportunity to shift her direction, tempo, or step pattern.
10. Give definite, strong, yet inconspicuous lead signals.
11. Plan ahead and try to make changes to coincide with the obvious accents and phrasing of the music. A change at the end of a musical phrase of four, eight, or sixteen measures is usually easier to lead and follow than one in the middle of a measure or phrase.

## Most Common Faults of Leaders

1. Haphazard and lazy dance position.
2. Watching either his feet or the floor.
3. Insufficient pressure of his hand on his partner's back, giving only a weak lead.
4. Taking too long a step forward or backward.

5. Stepping diagonally sideward when moving either forward or backward so that his feet are too far apart.
6. Stepping forward with the heel first.
7. Stepping with the toes turned out rather than with the feet parallel to each other, which usually causes him to step on the woman's feet.
8. Keeping his knees stiff, which causes a sharp bump into the floor at each step.
9. Inattention to the rhythm and/or tempo of the music.
10. Unnecessary tension in the shoulders and arms.
11. Bending forward toward his partner, causing her to lose her balance backward.

### Improving the Leader's Skills

A leader will give more assured leadership if he knows that he can do the steps in one place, turning, and through space. When he differentiates dance rhythms, recognizes changes in tempo, and has some sense of the uniqueness of each dance, he is even closer to success. When he can assume an efficient and balanced dance position and actually lead his partner in the steps he knows, then he is a ballroom dancer. Greater assurance comes only with practice. Lack of assurance only convinces both leader and follower that he will fail.

The following exercises are designed to improve leading skill.

1. Assume a good dance position, then drop your partner's right hand and let your left hand hang easily at your side. Now lead with your right hand only. Change directions, stop, start, turn, change into open position, and resume closed position. Don't talk your partner into the step; *lead* her with your right hand alone.
2. Assume a good dance position, then remove your right hand from your partner's waist, dropping it to your side, and have her drop her left hand to her side. Now lead with your left hand only. Change directions, stop, start, turn, change into open position, and resume closed position. Again, don't talk; *lead* your partner with your left hand alone.

After leading with only one hand, it will seem easier when you again assume the regular dance position and can use both hands to give lead indications. Try to remember then how forceful you had to be using only one hand.

### FOLLOWING

It is difficult to analyze just what makes "good following," but some of the more important factors are an ability to cooperate, sensitivity to the leader's task, an ability to adapt to other people's ideas, and graceful acceptance of the role of follower. Perhaps the most important tasks are to maintain good body alignment, correct dance position, and an easy, pleasant relationship to one's partner.

Cues for Good Following

1. Support your own weight without leaning on your partner.
2. Relax, and be ready to be led. Don't resist your partner's lead.
3. Remember that you do not step simultaneously with your partner, but just after his step.
4. Step directly backward *from the hip* to avoid bumping your partner's thigh.
5. Transfer your weight cleanly from one foot to the other, keeping on the balls of your feet.
6. Learn as many steps as possible and then practice them by yourself. Imagine you have a partner leading you.
7. Get as much experience as possible dancing with different partners and following their leads.
8. Keep your shoulders parallel to those of your partner.
9. Do not lean forward or backward from the hips.
10. Look at your partner or up and out at the world, not at the floor or your feet.
11. Develop perfect balance and learn to glide smoothly in response to your partner's lead.
12. Do not criticize or attempt to teach or lead your partner. Follow his lead even if you are convinced he is wrong.

Most Common Faults of Followers

1. Tension in her shoulders and arms.
2. Stepping backward from the knee rather than the hip.
3. Refusing to be led.
4. Twisting her shoulders away, so that they are not parallel to her partner's.
5. Leaning on her partner or forcing him to support her arms.
6. Watching the floor or her feet.
7. Insisting on her own choice of tempo, rhythm, direction, and step—pushing her partner around!

Improving the Follower's Skills

The follower must know the basic steps of each dance. Although the man leads the woman through variations of the basic steps, her knowledge of the foundation patterns permits her to follow his lead with intelligence and poise. She should practice the basic patterns of all dances without a partner, but using the proper posture, placement of hands, etc., as though he were there. She must not, however, develop the habit of practicing a set routine; each leader will vary his sequences.

A follower should not resist her partner's leading, but rather let him guide her through *his* movements. She should try to develop a sensitivity to his hand and body cues, so that he does not literally have to push and pull her through the steps. She must *never* try to follow a partner by looking at his feet.

All too frequently a woman will blame her partner if he steps on her toe. In most cases this occurs because the woman stepped backward from the *knee* rather than the hip. As she dances, she must stretch her entire leg backward, forward, or sideward. Her partner will prevent her from taking too long a step when dancing on a crowded floor.

The following exercises are designed to improve following skill.

1. Stand alone, with your eyes closed, arms at your sides. Relax as you sway slightly forward and back. Increase the sway until you tip off balance into a step either forward or backward. Repeat this several times until you can readily identify the point where you almost, but not quite, step. Try this with different kinds of dance music. Keep reminding yourself to find that point of balance when you assume the dance position with a partner. Resist the actual step; *wait* for the lead.

2. Lift your shoulders as high as you can, and let them drop. Circle your head forward, sideward, backward, and sideward; then reverse the direction. Lift your shoulders high again, and let them drop. Lean over from the waist, and let your arms and head hang like "wet spaghetti." Stand up, shake your hands vigorously, then drop them to your sides. Breathe deeply and evenly.

Good dance posture can be achieved by lifting the abdominal muscles very slightly and permitting the base of the pelvis to tilt forward a small amount at the same time. This should be done subtly, without creating muscular tension in the abdominal or pelvic area. Maintain your own weight, relax your shoulders, and *wait*. Keep reminding yourself of position, relaxation, and readiness.

*4*

# The American Waltz

In Austria, peasant dances in 3/4 time, called ländlers, existed as far back as the Middle Ages. They were popular at weddings, christenings, and folk festivals. The ländler is still popular as a folk dance in many sections of that and neighboring countries.

Prior to the French Revolution, the elaborate dance styles of the French court had dominated all of Europe. At the conclusion of the Revolution, Austria became the focal point of European musical and literary culture. Interest in her native dances increased, and the ländler moved from the rural areas into the drawing rooms of the elite, where it underwent considerable refinement and polishing. The name was changed to walzer, signifying sliding or gliding, and later the word was shortened to waltz as it became more popular throughout Europe.

The waltz was the first dance to use the closed position for any extended period of time, and because of this it was subjected to severe criticism and condemnation by both civic and church authorities. In many areas, the waltz was banned from public ballrooms for many years. (The storm of protests was not unlike the one rock 'n' roll dances encountered at their introduction in the early 1960s.)

The overwhelming popularity of the waltz eventually overcame the protests and restrictions placed on it. The closed face-to-face position became standard for ballroom dancing and has been used in the majority of dances developed since that era.

In Vienna, as the popularity of the waltz increased, so did its tempo. Johann

Strauss, Jr. (1825–1899), who succeeded his father as "waltz king of Vienna," increased the number of metronome beats per measure, and the Viennese waltz, as it came to be known to the world, demanded greater skill and endurance than the earlier, slower-tempo version. The Viennese waltz reigned supreme in the ballroom until the advent of World War I, when anything reflecting Germanic culture became anathema to parts of Europe and the United States.

Among dancers, however, the waltz was too popular to be discarded entirely. In the United States, new melodies replaced the Viennese ones, and the tempo was again decreased to an even three beats. An attempt was made to change the name of the dance to the Boston, but it eventually acquired the title *American waltz*. Exhibition dance teams, such as Irene and Vernon Castle, introduced new figures that could not have been performed in the rapidly accelerated tempo of the Viennese mode.

## STYLING

The American waltz requires good posture for both partners. Each must support his own weight in the closed position. To create the illusion of gliding, the dancers' feet remain close to the floor; steps originate from the hip, not from the knee.

The bodies of the dancers fall and rise subtly as they follow the accents of the music. This is accomplished by stepping flatly on the sole of the foot and slightly relaxing the knee at the accented first beat of the measure. On the following two beats, the dancers lift themselves, beginning from within the middle body, to rise lightly on the balls of their feet.

With only rare exceptions, the closed position is maintained throughout the dance. The man must lead the woman decisively, and in the turning sequences he must keep her directly in front of him at all times. All progressive figures flow forward in a counterclockwise line of direction around the dancing area.

## RHYTHM

Waltz music is written in 3/4 time, with three equal beats to the measure.

The first note of each measure is stressed, or emphasized. Dancers must learn to hear the stressed note, which indicates the count of 1. In the waltz, each count has a related foot movement. Despite the stress, however, each note is of equal duration. The waltz is the only dance that cannot be counted in combinations of slow and quick counts.

## FIGURES

### The Waltz Box (or Square)

In the waltz, the box (or square) is the foundation on which all other figures are based. While a box figure is common to many dances, the rhythm and styling of the waltz differ from those of other dances. The foot pattern consists of a series of three changes of weight in a triangular form. Placing two of the triangles together, one beginning forward and the other backward (or vice versa), produces a box or square pattern. Both men and women use the same directions for the initial practice exercise *without* partners.

#### The Waltz Box—Forward Half

|  | Count |
|---|---|
| Step fwd on LF | 1 |
| Bring RF fwd passing near LF & then step out to right side on RF | 2 |
| Close LF to RF & change wt to LF | 3 |

#### The Waltz Box—Backward Half

|  | Count |
|---|---|
| Step bkwd on RF | 1 |
| Bring LF bkwd passing near RF & then step out to left side on LF | 2 |
| Close RF to LF & change wt to RF | 3 |

As each foot takes a step, full weight is placed on it. At count 2, a small arc, or semicircular movement, is made with the leg as it swings forward or backward and out to the side.

Without regard to styling, the students should walk through both figures until they comprehend them. The most frequent error occurs on count 3, when students fail to transfer their weight to the foot taking that count.

Next, reverse the exercise, so that the students begin the waltz square leading backward with the right foot on count 1.

Note that one triangle, the forward half, begins with the *toe* of the left foot leading *forward*. The other, or backward half, begins with the *heel* of the right foot leading *backward*. This is important when the men and women are ready to dance together in closed position and in later development of turning figures.

### The Fall and Rise

After the pattern of the waltz square has become familiar, the fall and rise of the body may be added. During practice of the exercise, students must retain good, but not stiff, posture. The middle body should remain controlled but not constricted. Both men and women may practice without partners.

### The Body Fall and Rise

|  | Count |
|---|---|
| Step fwd flat on LF, letting left knee bend very slightly; full body wt is over LF | 1 |
| Step to right side with RF, making arc movement; as wt is transferred to RF, lift body slightly so that only fwd part of foot is resting on floor; make lift from middle or diaphragm area of body | 2 |
| Close LF to RF, retaining lift in body, & transferring wt to fwd part of LF | 3 |

Have the students reverse the figure by stepping backward on the right foot on the accented beat. The sole of the right shoe should be flat on the floor and the right knee bent slightly. Continue counts 2 and 3, the backward half of the waltz square, lifting the body and sustaining the lift for those two counts. The sequence can be cued verbally: "Flat, lift, lift."

To gain coordination of footwork and body movements, let the students practice individually to a recording of moderate tempo. Then they may take partners and practice the waltz square in closed ballroom position. The man must lead the woman into the exact counterpart of his footwork; as he steps forward he leads her into stepping backward. "Step, side, close," is a useful verbal cue to direct the footwork.

Reverse the exercise, having the man begin by stepping backward with his right foot. The figure may be started in either manner. The students should be given sufficient practice in both to use them adroitly.

The waltz square is a key to all that will follow in the dance and should be thoroughly understood by the dancers before new figures are introduced. This means the students must grasp the proper fall and rise of the body, correct timing with the rhythm, and accurate use of leading or following techniques.

## The Travel or Pursuit Waltz

To travel in the waltz, the same triangular patterns that formed the half-square are used. The important difference is that the triangles do not move alternately forward and backward but rather in one direction around the dancing area. The traveling figure is frequently termed the *pursuit waltz*.

For practice, have both men and women face the line of direction without partners and use the same footwork.

### The Pursuit Waltz (Travel Waltz)

|  | Count | Weight |
|---|---|---|
| Step fwd on LF | 1 | flat |
| Step fwd & to right side (making arc) on RF | 2 | lift |

*continued*

| | | |
|---|---|---|
| Close LF to RF & change wt | 3 | lift |
| | | |
| Step fwd on RF | 1 | flat |
| Step fwd & to left side (making arc) on LF | 2 | lift |
| Close RF to LF & change wt | 3 | lift |

To lend a little additional styling while practicing the traveling figure, have the students take a comfortably long step forward on each count of 1. The dancers should experience the feeling of moving from the hip rather than from the knee or ankle. Verbally this may be cued, "Reach, side, close."

When the forward pursuit waltz has become familiar, have the students turn their backs to the line of direction and reverse the figure. They will still be moving in the traditional counterclockwise path around the room but will be traveling backward. The long, reaching step on the count of 1 should be used again.

Next, students practice the pursuit waltz with partners until it is comfortable. Begin by having the man face the line of direction. As he moves forward, he leads the woman into the counterpart of his footwork so that she travels backward.

After sufficient practice, reverse the positions so that the man has his back to the line of direction. He will then travel backward and the woman forward. While it is difficult for a man to lead with authority and control in this position until he has gained experience, it should be practiced for a few measures to emphasize that it is permissible for the man to travel backward in the waltz if he so desires.

For an easy practice sequence, alternate four measures of the waltz square with four measures of the pursuit waltz. Have the students practice the sequence until they can move from one figure into the other without difficulty. Observe whether rhythm, fall and rise, and leading or following techniques are being heeded, as well as footwork patterns.

Allow the students to make their own sequences by combining any number of measures of the waltz square with any number of the pursuit waltz. Because the responsibility of creating the sequence falls to the men, they must concentrate on giving clear and positive leads if they expect their partners to respond properly. In a two-figure sequence, the men will soon experience the correct use of their hands and bodies to lead effectively.

## The Waltz Turn

Turning figures in the waltz may revolve in either direction. In a *left* turn, the dancers move in a *counterclockwise* direction; a *right* turn revolves them in a *clockwise* direction.

In operating an automobile, the driver learns that he must turn the wheels to the left to make a left turn or to the right to make a right turn. The same principle applies to making a turn in dancing. For the beginning dancer, the easiest way to turn to the left is to point the toe of his left foot outward to the left as he makes the first step. He then continues to turn toward that direction. To make a right turn, the dancer leads with the toe of his right foot turned toward the right. When the turn is performed in place it is known as a *box turn*. It is essentially the same as the waltz square, but with the development of a turning movement.

Working individually, have both men and women walk through the counter-clockwise box turn.

### The Box Turn, Counterclockwise (Quarter-Turn)

|  | Count |
|---|---|
| Step fwd on LF, toe turned out to left, making 1/4 turn left (CCW) | 1 |
| Step swd, making arc as in waltz square, on RF | 2 |
| Close LF to RF & change wt to LF | 3 |
| Step bkwd on RF, toe turned *in* to left (heel out), making 1/4 turn left (CCW) | 1 |
| Step swd, making arc, on LF | 2 |
| Close RF to LF & change wt to RF | 3 |

If the dancer has been making a quarter-turn on each three counts, it will take four measures, or twelve beats, to make a complete revolution. For beginning students, the degree of the turn should not be overstressed as long as its direction is correct. The dancers should observe that the count of 1 is important in establishing the direction of the turn, whether the first step is taken *forward* with the toe turned *out* or *backward* with the toe turned *in*.

Have the students repeat the exercise, adding the correct "Flat, lift, lift," body motion. The first count may also be accented by reaching forward or backward with a long step. The directional cue "Turn, side, close" may be used with this exercise.

After sufficient individual practice with music, the dancers should rejoin their partners in closed position. In turning figures in the waltz, the man must keep his partner directly in front of him as they revolve together. A common error is for the man to attempt to step around his partner.

In closed position, the woman performs the exact counterpart of the man's steps. As he steps forward on his left foot with toe turned out, he must lead her into stepping backward on her right foot with her toe turned in (heel out). The box turn revolves in place, in either direction. The dancers should not attempt to make the figure travel.

After the students have had sufficient practice doing box turns to the left (counterclockwise), make a practice sequence of four measures of pursuit waltz alternating with four measures of box turns revolving left. Then let the men lead their own sequences of the same two figures.

Without partners, the students should walk through the box turn to the *right* (revolving clockwise). Both men and women step forward on their right feet with toes turned out to the right. The directions are the reverse of those given for the box turn to the left. Dancers usually find the turn to the right more difficult to accomplish, and it may be necessary to spend more time upon it.

## Changing Directions of Turns

There are two methods of changing the direction of a turning figure in the waltz. Experienced dancers accomplish the change by using an odd number of measures—three, five, seven—turning to the left. As the man's right foot becomes free, he shifts the direction of the turn to the right by quickly leading forward with his right foot pointed out (instead of backward and pointed in).

With beginning dancers it is easier to use one of two figures as a connecting link. One is known as the *waltz balance,* and the other is the *waltz hesitation.* Both retain the rhythm of the waltz, but the footwork varies from the basic triangular pattern. The students may use whichever is most comfortable, but they should be familiar with both.

### The Waltz Balance

| Man | Count | Woman |
|---|---|---|
| Step fwd on LF | 1 | Step bkwd on RF |
| Close RF to LF, rising on ball of RF | 2 | Close LF to RF, rising on ball of RF |
| Transfer wt to LF in place, maintaining lift in body | 3 | Transfer wt to RF in place, maintaining lift in body |
| Step bkwd on RF | 1 | Step fwd on LF |
| Close LF to RF, rising on ball of LF | 2 | Close RF to LF, rising on ball of RF |
| Transfer wt to RF in place, maintaining lift in body | 3 | Transfer wt to LF in place, maintaining lift in body |

### The Waltz Hesitation

| Man | Count | Woman |
|---|---|---|
| Step fwd on LF | 1 | Step bkwd on RF |
| Close toe of RF to LF, making slight body lift, but *without* changing wt | 2 | Close toe of LF to RF, making slight body lift, but *without* changing wt |
| Hold same position | 3 | Hold same position |

| | | |
|---|---|---|
| Step bkwd on RF | 1 | Step fwd on LF |
| Close toe of LF to RF, making slight body lift, but *without* changing wt | 2 | Close toe of RF to LF, making slight body lift, but *without* changing wt |
| Hold same position | 3 | Hold same position |

Either figure may be performed beginning forward, backward, or from side to side. Steps should be small.

## The Extended Turn

The extended turn uses the basic box turn but develops it into a progressive step by using a half-turn in place of the quarter-turn.

For the initial practice, dancers should move to one end of the room and perform the extended turn in a straight line down the length of the room. Both men and women should use the same footwork in the beginning without partners.

### The Extended Turn, Counterclockwise (Half-turn)

| | Count |
|---|---|
| Step fwd on LF in LOD, making 1/4 turn to left (toe turned *out*) | 1 |
| Step swd on RF in LOD, continuing 1/4 turn to left (dancers should now have backs to LOD, having made a complete 1/2 turn) | 2 |
| Close LF to RF & change wt to LF | 3 |
| Step bkwd on RF in LOD, making 1/4 turn to left (toe turned *in*) | 1 |
| Step swd on LF in LOD, continuing 1/4 turn to left (dancers should now be facing LOD) | 2 |
| Close RF to LF & change wt to RF | 3 |

Practice will be required to keep the extended turn moving in a straight line. A strong, definite step on the count of 1, whether leading forward or backward, will help. After sufficient individual practice, partners may practice together in closed position. The woman will perform the counterpart of the man's steps. The man must keep his partner directly in front of him throughout the turning figure.

To help avoid dizziness, keep the eyes at normal eye level. (See the advice on avoiding dizziness in chapter 5.)

The clockwise extended turn (to the right) simply reverses the left turn. Again, it should be practiced individually before partners try it together. Most beginning dancers find it more difficult than the counterclockwise turn, so it may require more practice time.

In making the extended turn figure the man must hold his partner securely with his right arm, keeping her directly in front of him; his hips and shoulders must always remain parallel to hers. With music of a fast tempo, the size of the steps must become *correspondingly smaller* than those used with a slower tempo. In making a series of extended turns, the appearance of the dancing couple will be enhanced if each partner pulls his or her shoulders slightly backward.

### The Diagonal Crossover

The diagonal crossover is an easy variant of the pursuit step that creates a graceful weaving pattern as it moves along. This figure should be restricted to use with slow waltz music; otherwise it loses its grace and dignity. It should be used as a traveling figure and not in place.

*The Diagonal Crossover*

| Man | Count | Woman |
|---|---|---|
| Step diag fwd on LF, crossing left leg between yourself and partner, so that your left hips are adjacent | 1 | Step diag bkwd on RF |
| Step swd to right on RF | 2 | Step swd to left on LF |
| Close LF to RF & change wt to LF | 3 | Close RF to LF & change wt to RF |
| Step diag fwd on RF, crossing right leg between yourself and partner, so that your right hips are adjacent | 1 | Step diag bkwd on LF |
| Step swd to left on LF | 2 | Step swd to right on RF |
| Close RF to LF & change wt to RF | 3 | Close LF to RF & change wt to LF |

On counts 2 and 3, the dancers turn slightly toward their partners, ending face to face on the final count. The man must lead his partner firmly into the crossover; she steps *diagonally* backward as he steps *diagonally* forward. The characteristic fall and rise of the body should be maintained. The figure may also be reversed, with the man leading backward. The diagonal crossing step must not be allowed to develop into a *dip.*

All figures of the waltz should create an impression of effortless gliding and turning to an even cadence. Dancers must maintain a proudly erect and dignified body carriage.

PRACTICE COMBINATIONS

For beginning dancers, a waltz of a moderate tempo is better than one that is too slow. A slow tempo requires sustaining the movements of the body, a difficult feat for inexperienced dancers.

The following combinations are suggested merely for practice; students should not be required to memorize them.

Combination 1

2 waltz balance (or 2 hesitation) figures, 1 fwd & 1 bkwd . . . . . 2 meas
4 pursuit figures, traveling . . . . . . . . . . . . . . . . 4 meas
2 complete waltz box figures, without turning . . . . . . . . 4 meas
2 complete waltz box figures, turning in place . . . . . . . . 4 meas
Repeat the sequence several times.

Combination 2

4 pursuit figures, traveling . . . . . . . . . . . . . . . . 4 meas
2 complete waltz boxes without turning . . . . . . . . . . 4 meas
4 pursuit figures, traveling . . . . . . . . . . . . . . . . 4 meas
2 complete waltz boxes turning in place . . . . . . . . . . 4 meas
Repeat the entire sequence.

Combination 3

1 waltz balance (or 1 hesitation) figure, fwd . . . . . . . . . 1 meas
2 complete waltz boxes, turning left (CCW) . . . . . . . . . 4 meas
1 waltz balance (or 1 hesitation) figure, fwd . . . . . . . . . 1 meas
2 complete waltz boxes, turning right (CW) . . . . . . . . . 4 meas
Repeat the sequence until the change of direction in the waltz box is familiar.

Combination 4

1 hesitation figure, fwd . . . . . . . . . . . . . . . . . 1 meas
2 complete waltz boxes, beginning with RF, bkwd . . . . . . 4 meas
1 hesitation figure, fwd, beginning with RF . . . . . . . . . 1 meas
8 pursuit figures, traveling . . . . . . . . . . . . . . . 8 meas
Repeat the entire sequence.

Combination 5

8 extended turns to left (CCW) . . . . . . . . . . . . . 8 meas
3 waltz balance (or 3 hesitation) figures . . . . . . . . . . 3 meas

8 extended turns to right (CW)   . . . . . . . . . . . . . 8 meas
3 waltz balance (or 3 hesitation) figures   . . . . . . . . . . 3 meas
Repeat the sequence until the change of direction in the extended turn is familiar.

## Combination 6

8 diagonal crossover figures   . . . . . . . . . . . . . . . 8 meas
3 waltz balance (or 3 hesitation) figures   . . . . . . . . . . 3 meas
8 pursuit figures, traveling   . . . . . . . . . . . . . . . 8 meas
3 waltz balance (or 3 hesitation) figures   . . . . . . . . . . 3 meas
Repeat until the sequence is familiar.

# 5

# The Fox Trot

In the late 1890s, American ballroom dancing consisted mostly of the fast Viennese waltz, or simply walking, in closed dance position, to march music. In the southern states, black musicians began to syncopate the march music by introducing an opposing divided beat against the regularly accented base. It was not long before this syncopation was picked up by dance orchestras, and the new music was termed *ragtime.* An entirely new style of dancing developed with it. The dignified walking of the march was transformed into grotesque holds with exaggerated body and arm movements. The dances bore such descriptive names as *turkey trot, grizzly bear, kangaroo hop, bunny hug,* and *harem glide.* Many were reputed to have originated in the dance halls of San Francisco's Barbary Coast and New York's Bowery, but they were quickly adopted by ardent dancers everywhere.

In 1913, a young vaudevillian named Harry Fox embellished his act in the New York theaters by dancing a "trot" around the stage with each of several attractive chorines. Harry Fox's "trot" was simple and spontaneous, but the dancing public was fascinated by his new interpretation of the popular ragtime rhythm. Dancing teachers quickly responded to the requests, and the stage version of the Fox "trot" was modified to meet the needs of the ballroom.

The fox trot underwent additional simplification as it passed through numerous dance crazes, but it remains one of the most standard and popular dances wherever dancing is performed. The music too has changed considerably since the ragtime era, becoming smoother and more flowing. Young dancers growing up in the rock 'n' roll era frequently call the fox trot the *slow dance.*

## STYLING

Closed position is generally used, but open positions may be taken at times to lend variety. Good posture should be maintained by both dancers, but the body must be relaxed and pliable. All steps use the *dancer's walk*—that is, the toe touches the floor before the heel is brought down. Although some figures may be performed in place, the fox trot generally moves freely around the dancing area, traveling in a counterclockwise direction.

Fox trot music still retains a slight syncopation, and the dancer's body frequently follows the rhythm with a slight bending and straightening of the knees. The music is played in a variety of moods, which the good dancer will also follow. A routine of steps that suits one musical selection may not comfortably fit another fox trot played in a different tempo or mood.

## RHYTHM

Fox trot music is written in 4/4 time, with four beats to the measure:

If a step were taken on each note in the measure, it would be counted "Quick, quick, quick, quick." The fox trot, however, is composed of varying combinations of quick and slow steps. The slow step is made by stepping on one count and holding the weight on that foot for the second count:

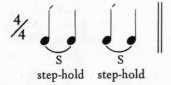

S          S
step-hold   step-hold

## FIGURES

### The Fox Trot Walk

The walking step is an important element in the fox trot and should be practiced sufficiently so that the transition from the slow to quick steps is made smoothly and confidently. Beginning dancers may practice a series of walking steps without partners before they assume the closed position.

Begin with all dancers around the room facing the counterclockwise line of direction. A series of *slow* steps—the step-hold figure—should be practiced; both men and women may begin with the same foot, so that the instructor can easily call the directions. The majority of fox trot music is accented on the first and third beats in each measure; the change of weight must be made on those accented counts. (For beginning dance students, use music in which these accents are clearly defined.) The dancer's body subtly follows the musical syncopation when using slow steps in the fox trot, relaxing or bending the knee of the standing leg slightly on the *unaccented* count. The bend must be extremely subtle; it is *sensed* by the dancers rather than being visible to an observer. Verbally, it may be counted, "Step-bend, step-bend."

Have the students practice a series of slow walking steps. Observe that the toe lead is used and that the movement originates from the hip. They must maintain good, but relaxed, posture and keep the bend barely perceptible.

In the *fast* walking step, there is one change of weight for each beat of music. Fast steps are never syncopated and are generally of shorter length than slow ones. The dance walk should be maintained, with feet kept close to the floor and the body properly erect.

After the students have practiced the fast walk, they may practice a simple combination of slow and quick figures. For example, alternate two measures of each, making a sequence of four slow steps, and eight quick steps. Verbally it may be counted, "Step-bend, step-bend, step-bend, step-bend; quick-quick, quick-quick, quick-quick, quick-quick."

After a brief, but sufficient, practice of the combination, let the students, still without partners, make their own combinations of quick and slow steps. Check that the changes of rhythm flow together without awkward pauses. Two quick steps equal one slow step, rhythmically, and in the fox trot two quick steps (or a multiple of two) are always made together.

Next, have the students turn their backs to the line of direction and briefly practice all the above sequences. Check that the toe lead is being used, and that the movement is from the hip.

Permit the dancers to take partners and repeat the same combinations in closed position. In the free combination of slow and quick walking steps, both partners will begin to sense the significance of leading and following (see chapter 3). The combinations need not be complex, but the man must decide what combinations to use, and the woman must learn to respond. In this simple practice combination, the woman should always perform the counterpart of the pattern directed by the man; that is, if he leads a step *forward* with his *left* foot, she will step *backward* with her *right* foot. (In the United States, it has become traditional for the man to begin all closed position dances with his left foot.) Have the students practice with the man moving *backward* in the line of direction, also.

## Fox Trot Two-Step

In the early 1900s, a popular dance was the two-step, a fast-moving combination of three changes of weight in 2/4 time. As the fox trot grew in popularity, the two-step combination became an intrinsic part of it, but in a smoother, slower

4/4 tempo. Like all the basic fox trot figures, the two-step is a combination of slow and quick steps. Two quick steps are taken on counts 1 and 2 of the measure; the slow step is taken on count 3 and held for count 4.

Q    Q    S

This pattern begins with one foot and then the other alternately. It may travel forward, backward, or from side to side, or it can turn in place.

First, students should practice the two-step combination without partners, each dancer facing the line of direction.

*The Two-Step*

|                          | Count | Rhythm |
|--------------------------|-------|--------|
| Step fwd on LF           | 1     | Q      |
| Step fwd on RF, near LF  | 2     | Q      |
| Step fwd on LF           | 3–4   | S      |
|                          |       |        |
| Step fwd on RF           | 1     | Q      |
| Step fwd on LF, near RF  | 2     | Q      |
| Step fwd on RF           | 3–4   | S      |

Verbally, the two-step is frequently cued: "Step, close, step."

Beginning dancers need to practice the two-step until they fully comprehend the structure and can perform it smoothly, without halting movements.

After sufficient practice in moving forward, the dancers may turn their backs to the line of direction and practice moving backward. The same quick, quick, slow sequence is used, but all steps are directed backward. A common error made by most beginning students is to take short, mincing steps backward.

After the students have practiced the two-step both forward and backward individually, permit them to take partners in closed position. First practice a series with the man facing the line of direction and the woman moving backward; then change so that the man's back is to the line of direction and the woman moves forward. In all initial practice sessions with a partner, the man must begin to grow more cognizant of his role as leader by thinking about the proper use of his hands and body, and not about the footwork alone.

## Side-to-Side Two-Step

The two-step is also performed from side to side.

### The Side-to-Side Two-Step

|  | Count | Rhythm |
|---|---|---|
| Step directly to left with LF | 1 | Q |
| Close RF to LF & change wt | 2 | Q |
| Step directly to left with LF | 3–4 | S |
| | | |
| Step directly to right with RF | 1 | Q |
| Close LF to RF & change wt | 2 | Q |
| Step directly to right with RF | 3–4 | S |

In closed position, the woman does the counterpart of the man's steps. The figure may also begin to the man's *right,* if he desires.

Because the side-to-side two-step remains in place, it is used principally when dancers find themselves in a crowded area where they cannot make progressive movements.

## The Canter

A footwork combination that has endured through the many changes of the fox trot's long history is the canter. This is a valuable foundation figure, because the footwork pattern alternates if it is used in a sequence of two or more measures.

### The Canter

|  | Count | Rhythm |
|---|---|---|
| Step fwd on LF | 1–2 | S |
| Step fwd on RF | 3–4 | S |
| Short step fwd on LF | 5 | Q |
| Short step fwd on RF | 6 | Q |
| Step fwd on LF | 7–8 | S |
| | | |
| Step fwd on RF | 1–2 | S |
| Step fwd on LF | 3–4 | S |
| Short step fwd on RF | 5 | Q |
| Short step fwd on LF | 6 | Q |
| Step fwd on RF | 7–8 | S |

Without partners, have the students briefly practice the basic figure, moving forward in the line of direction; then they may turn their backs to the line of direction and reverse the sequence, moving backward.

With partners in closed position, the students then repeat the same exercise; the woman uses the counterpart of the man's steps.

## The Twinkle

The canter pattern may be developed into a *twinkle* variation by making a change of direction on the quick steps.

### The Twinkle

| | Count | Rhythm |
|---|---|---|
| Step fwd on LF | 1–2 | S |
| Step fwd on RF | 3–4 | S |
| Short step fwd on LF | 5 | Q |
| Close RF to LF & change wt | 6 | Q |
| Step bkwd on LF | 7–8 | S |
| | | |
| Step bkwd on RF | 1–2 | S |
| Step bkwd on LF | 3–4 | S |
| Short step bkwd on RF | 5 | Q |
| Close LF to RF & change wt | 6 | Q |
| Step fwd on RF | 7–8 | S |

In closed position, the woman uses the counterpart of the man's steps.

## The Box (or Square) Figure

There are *two* combinations of footwork that result in a box or square floor pattern, and both are commonly used in the fox trot. For simplification in identification, one will be termed the *primary box* and the other the *secondary box*. Both are used extensively, but each has its own rhythmic pattern and method of initiation. In practicing both figures, students need to visualize their feet moving in a box or square. Each figure should be performed by the dancers without partners until they are proficient in it.

The primary box figure follows a "slow, quick, quick" rhythm.

### The Primary Box

| | Count | Rhythm |
|---|---|---|
| Step fwd on LF | 1–2 | S |
| Step fwd & to side on RF | 3 | Q |
| Close LF to RF & change wt | 4 | Q |

| | | |
|---|---|---|
| Step bkwd on RF | 1–2 | S |
| Step bkwd & to side on LF | 3 | Q |
| Close RF to LF & change wt | 4 | Q |

Each four counts creates a triangular pattern; it takes *two* of these patterns to finish a box or square (see chapter 2). The figure may also be initiated with the man stepping *backward* on his right foot on the count of 1 to create the first triangle, and then *forward* on the count of 5 to complete the square.

Students may practice the figure individually; then they take partners in closed position with the woman performing the counterpart of the man's steps.

The secondary box figure follows a "quick, quick, slow" rhythm.

*The Secondary Box*

| | Count | Rhythm |
|---|---|---|
| Short step swd on LF | 1 | Q |
| Close RF to LF & change wt | 2 | Q |
| Step fwd on LF | 3–4 | S |
| Short step swd on RF | 1 | Q |
| Close LF to RF & change wt | 2 | Q |
| Step bkwd on RF | 3–4 | S |

The man may also initiate this figure by stepping sideward on his *right* foot on the count of 1. The woman uses the counterpart of the man's footwork in closed position.

## The Hesitation

The hesitation is an easy figure that adds variety, serves as a connecting link between other figures, and is useful in a crowded area. It may be used in different ways by changing the direction of movement. In the most common variant, it remains in place, alternately stepping forward and backward (or vice versa).

*The Hesitation*

| | Count | Rhythm |
|---|---|---|
| Step fwd on LF | 1 | Q |
| Bring RF fwd to LF, *without* changing wt | 2 | Q |
| Step bkwd on RF | 3 | Q |
| Bring LF bkwd to RF, *without* changing wt | 4 | Q |

The toe of the free foot may rest on the floor beside the standing foot to maintain balance, but without taking on full weight. The figure may be repeated several times, as desired. In closed position, the woman's steps are the counterpart of the man's.

Another variant uses the same pattern but directs the movements from side to side. The figure may also be used as a progressive pattern, taking a series of steps either forward or backward.

## Turning

To turn an automobile, the driver turns the wheels in the direction he wishes to move. In dancing, the feet serve the same purpose as the wheels—that is, they *lead* the direction of the turn.

Some turns remain in place; others travel. The degree of the turn determines that factor. In practice, both men and women should rehearse the same sequences individually before dancing with partners.

## The Primary Box Turn, Counterclockwise (Quarter-Turn)

The majority of beginning dancers find that the easiest direction in which to make a turning figure is to their *left,* or counterclockwise. In a quarter-turn in place, the box figure loses its square form, but the basic premise remains the same.

Working individually, have both men and women walk through the figure. Using the four walls of the room as focal points will frequently help them keep a sense of direction.

*The Primary Box Turn, Counterclockwise*

|  | Count | Rhythm |
|---|---|---|
| Step fwd on LF, *toe* turned *out* to left, making 1/4 turn left (CCW) | 1–2 | S |
| Step to side on RF (step should not be too wide) | 3 | Q |
| Close LF to RF & change wt to LF | 4 | Q |
| Step bkwd on RF, toe turned *in* to left (heel turned *out*), making 1/4 turn left (CCW) | 1–2 | S |
| Step to side on LF (not too wide) | 3 | Q |
| Close RF to LF & change wt to RF | 4 | Q |

To complete the turn, repeat the above sequence. It takes *four* measures of 4/4 music to complete a full turn in place. In a fast fox trot, the feet may continue to pivot on the "quick" counts, but it is the "slow" counts that control the direction and degree of the turn. The slow counts should be made decisively and with authority, especially by the leader. Although it is the toe that points the direction of the turn, the entire leg should be brought into action from the hip downward, not from the ankle.

After sufficient individual practice with music, the students may rejoin partners in closed position. For any turning figure, both dancers need to remain close together, but neither should attempt to lean on the other or pull his or her partner off balance. The man should hold the woman firmly but gently.

The woman will perform the exact counterpart of the man's steps. As he steps *forward* on his left foot (with toe turned out), he must lead her into stepping *backward* on her right foot (toe turned *in,* heel out). The counterclockwise turn may also be initiated by the man leading *backward* with his *right* foot, in which case the woman steps *forward* onto her *left* foot. A good leader should be able to initiate the turn in either manner, but it will require practice.

In making turns, a common error is for one partner to attempt to step around the other. Partners must remain directly in front of one another, with hips and shoulders parallel throughout the turn.

The Primary Box Turn, Clockwise (Quarter-Turn)

The box turn to the *right,* or clockwise, is the reverse of the left turn. It should be practiced first by leading forward on the *right* foot, pointing the toe to the right to make a quarter turn.

*The Primary Box Turn, Clockwise*

|  | Count | Rhythm |
|---|---|---|
| Step fwd on RF, *toe* turned *out* to right, making 1/4 turn right (CW) | 1–2 | S |
| Step to side on LF (not too wide) | 3 | Q |
| Close RF to LF & change wt to RF | 4 | Q |
| Step bkwd on LF, toe turned *in* to right (heel turned *out*), making 1/4 turn right (CW) | 1–2 | S |
| Step to side on RF (not too wide) | 3 | Q |
| Close LF to RF & change wt to LF | 4 | Q |

Continue for four more counts, repeating the sequence and leading to the *right* on counts 1 and 3, to complete a full turn in place.

After sufficient practice individually, partners may practice the turn together. The principle remains the same as in the counterclockwise turn. A common error with beginners is for the man to place his right arm too far around the woman's back, thus inhibiting the degree of the turn.

A clockwise turn may also be initiated by the man leading *backward* with his left foot while making a quarter-turn to the right. The woman will use the counterpart of the man's steps. Both methods of beginning a right, or clockwise, turn should be practiced.

Generally, the fox trot progresses rapidly around the dancing area. For that reason box turns, which remain in a small area, should be used sparingly, especially if the room is crowded, because they may impede the action of other couples.

### The Secondary Box Turn

Turns in place (either counterclockwise or clockwise) may be accomplished using the "quick, quick, slow" rhythm in the same manner as the primary rhythm.

*The Secondary Box Turn, Counterclockwise*

|  | Count | Rhythm |
|---|---|---|
| Step fwd on LF, *toe* turned *out* to left, making 1/4 turn (CCW) | 1 | Q |
| Step to side on RF (not too wide) | 2 | Q |
| Close LF to RF & change wt to LF | 3–4 | S |
| Step bkwd on RF, toe turned *in* to left (heel turned *out*), making 1/4 turn (CCW) | 1 | Q |
| Step to side on LF (not too wide) | 2 | Q |
| Close RF to LF & change wt to RF | 3–4 | S |

The sequence is repeated two more times to make a complete revolution in place.

Like the primary turn, the secondary box turn may also be developed into a right, or *clockwise*, turn, by directing the steps to the right. Again, the dancers should practice it individually before they try it in closed position. This turn need not be taught until the more basic figures have been mastered. Dancers with some experience have less difficulty with it than those who are complete novices.

### Progressive Turns (Half-Turns)

Both box figures may be developed into turns that progress in a straight line of direction as the dancers revolve. This is accomplished by making a *half*-turn in place of the quarter-revolution.

To teach the progressive turn, it is wise to start the students at one end of the room so that they can progress in a straight line to the other end. This is less confusing than having the dancers move in a large circle. Initially both men and women should practice the same footwork.

### The Progressive Turn

|  | Count | Rhythm |
|---|---|---|
| Facing LOD (opposite end of room), step fwd on LF, *toe* turned *out* to left, making 1/2 turn left (CCW) so that *back* is to LOD. | 1-2 | S |
| Short step bkwd on RF | 3 | Q |
| Close LF to RF & change wt to LF | 4 | Q |
| With *back* to LOD, step bkwd on RF, *toe* turned *in* to left (heel turned *out*), making 1/2 turn left (CCW) to *face* LOD | 1-2 | S |
| Short step fwd on LF | 3 | Q |
| Close RF to LF & change wt to RF | 4 | Q |

To move in a straight line (and later in a large circle) it is vital that the steps on counts 1 and 3 are taken completely toward the line of direction (whether forward or backward). More force is required to turn the body the half-revolution than the quarter-turn. However, dancers must not acquire the habit of forcing the turn by "whipping" with their shoulders and arms. Generally, the leading steps of a half-turn (counts 1 and 3) are slightly longer than those needed for a quarter-turn. Even though the toes are pointed toward the direction of the turn, the actual turn is not made until the foot is on the floor; the leg on the leading count steps toward the line of direction.

Without partners, the dancers may practice a series of progressive turns, moving from one end of the room to the other, until they master the figure. Then, with partners in closed position, have them continue to move in a straight line the length of the room. The woman uses the counterpart of the man's steps. After they have had sufficient practice in a straight line, place the couples in the traditional circle around the floor, and have them briefly practice moving in the counterclockwise line of direction. Observe that they do not make small circles in place but rather use their turns to travel in one large circle.

With inexperienced dancers, turning frequently produces some dizziness. Most commonly this is because the dancers are looking down at the floor or their feet. It is better to keep the eyes at normal eye level. One device is to concentrate on the back of one's own left hand (leaders must be careful not to run into another couple while doing this). A more advanced method, which requires considerable practice, is termed *spotting*. Each dancer looks ("spots") toward the line of direction and focuses there until he *has* to turn his head, after which he again focuses in the same direction. Because the head is turned more slowly than the body, it must be quickly brought around to refocus; care must be taken not to snap the neck too vigorously. As dancers gain experience in turning they generally find that dizziness becomes less of a problem.

After practicing the half-turn to the left, it should be developed into a *right* turn. Again, the principle is the same as that of the quarter-turn to the right, but a half-revolution is made so that the dancers travel.

### Changing Directions in a Turn

As fox trot dancers gain experience over a period of time they should be able to reverse the direction of the turns as they progress forward in the line of direction. This change of direction is effected by inserting an *odd* number of hesitation figures (usually one or three) between the counterclockwise and clockwise turns. A simple practice sequence consists of four half-turns to the left (CCW) beginning with the left foot (8 counts); three hesitation steps in place (6 counts), beginning either forward or backward on the left foot and ending with the right foot free; four half-turns to the right (CW) progressing in the line of direction; and three hesitation steps to free the left foot again. In closed position, as always, the woman does the counterpart of the man's steps.

### PRACTICE COMBINATIONS

Eventually, students should try to create their own combinations and fit them to the various moods of fox trot music. For beginning dancers, however, it is often advisable to offer a few practice combinations that include all the step patterns. It would be detrimental to the spontaneous quality so desirable in the fox trot to force students to memorize set sequences of figures in this dance, however.

### Combination 1

| | |
|---|---:|
| 8 slow dance walks | 4 meas |
| 2 complete box steps in place | 4 meas |
| 8 slow dance walks | 4 meas |
| 2 complete box turns | 4 meas |
| Repeat the entire sequence several times. | |

### Combination 2

| | |
|---|---:|
| 2 complete canter walks | 4 meas |
| 4 hesitation steps | 2 meas |
| 8 two-steps | 4 meas |
| 4 hesitation steps | 2 meas |
| Repeat the entire sequence several times. | |

Combination 3

> 8 two-steps . . . . . . . . . . . . . . . . . . . . 4 meas
> 2 side-to-side two-steps . . . . . . . . . . . . . . . 2 meas
> 2 complete canters . . . . . . . . . . . . . . . . . . 4 meas
> 2 complete secondary box steps in place . . . . . . . . . . 4 meas
> Repeat the sequence several times.

Combination 4

> 2 primary box turns . . . . . . . . . . . . . . . . . 4 meas
> 2 twinkle variations of canter . . . . . . . . . . . . . 4 meas
> 4 progressive turns (half turns) traveling . . . . . . . . . 4 meas
> 8 slow dance walks . . . . . . . . . . . . . . . . . 4 meas
> Repeat the sequence several times.

In the United States, it has become traditional for the man to take the initial step of all closed position dances with his left foot. That does not mean that all combinations should begin on that foot, however. Good dancers must learn to begin subsequent combinations with either foot. The fox trot has an element of jauntiness, but the footwork and body rhythm must be blended into a varied and harmonious whole that affords the dancers many hours of pleasure without undue fatigue or strain.

# 6

# The Argentine Tango

*Two* dances carry the name *tango*. This fact has compounded confusion among both dancers and musicians for a long time. Other than the name, the two have little in common.

Spain was the home of the original tango. In that country it is an exhibition dance performed by a solo dancer who directs the sharp accents of heel rhythms, snapping fingers, and flowing arm movements into a blend of both classical and gypsy Iberian dance. The music for the Spanish tango has a sharp staccato rhythm and is usually in 2/4 time.

In contrast, the social dance used on ballroom floors owes its origin to the gauchos, the sturdy cowboys of the Argentine pampas. Both the dance and the music have undergone extensive modifications since their inception, dated by historians in the 1880s. In Argentina, the original dance bore the name *El Baile con Corte,* meaning "the dance with a stop."

About 1910, the Argentine dance was taken to Europe where exhibition dance teams were beginning to be popular in fashionable cafes. It was probably there that the Argentine dance acquired the name of the Spanish dance and countless innovations were made in the steps and styling. By about 1913, when the tango reached the United States, the original music had been supplanted by a throbbing habanera rhythm, and steps more like the French apache dance than the controlled, catlike movements of the gauchos and their partners. The dancing team of Irene and Vernon Castle is credited with returning the dance to the more modest styling and rhythm of the Argentine original.

STYLING

Clothing often plays an important role in imparting a style of movement to dancers. The gauchos dressed in heavy, flowing pantaloons, thick leather boots adorned with metal spurs, and wide leather belts laden with silver ornaments. Their partners wore long, heavily ruffled skirts over several underskirts of heavy cotton. This apparel precluded light and bouncy movements and instilled a controlled, feline quality which tango dancers still try to achieve.

In the tango, dancers use an erect, but not stiff, posture. Neither partner leans on the other for support. Most steps originate from the hips, not the knees. They are made smoothly without any bouncing or syncopation of the body.

The steps resemble normal walking steps more closely than those in other dances; dancers are even permitted to lead with the heel rather than the toe, occasionally. The feet remain close to the floor in smooth, gliding movements. In slow sequences, dancers must learn to sustain the movement within their bodies between steps.

RHYTHM

Argentine tango music may be composed in either 2/4 or 4/4 meter. Both time signatures give the same easily distinguished beat to the music; the only difference is that one is played faster than the other. For simplicity in counting, the examples in this chapter will be in 4/4 time.

While all social dances are danced to the *beat* of the music, the tango has the added factor of being danced to the *phrase*. A complete musical phrase in the tango consists of eight measures of music, each measure containing four beats. Each complete phrase, however, is broken up into four subphrases of two measures each. Each subphrase contains eight counts, and it is on these eight counts (or beats) that the basic figures of the tango are built.

Beginning students need to learn to distinguish the musical subphrases in order to make their dance pattern phrases coincide. The secret of distinguishing the subphrases lies in the melodic line. The melody for each subphrase is completed, or comes to a pause, on the count of 8. It then picks up again on the following count of 1. The dancers must learn to distinguish both the musical phrase (or subphrase) and the underlying rhythmic beat.

FIGURES

The Tango March (Basic Figure)

The tango march is used in many different ways to create "new" figures without actually altering the rhythm or footwork. In all variations, the woman uses the counterpart of the man's steps.

*The Tango March*

| | Count | Rhythm |
|---|---|---|
| Long step fwd on LF | 1-& | S |
| Long step fwd on RF | 2-& | S |
| Short step fwd on LF | 3 | Q |
| Short step fwd on RF | & | Q |
| Long step fwd on LF | 4-& | S |
| Long step fwd on RF | 5-& | S |
| Long step fwd on LF | 6-& | S |
| Short step fwd on RF | 7 | Q |
| Short step fwd on LF | & | Q |
| Long step fwd on RF | 8-& | S |

The footwork alternates with each measure; if the dancer begins with the left foot on count 1, then count 5 will begin on the right foot.

Dancers should practice the sequence individually, men beginning with the left foot and women with the right. They may also practice the figure moving backward.

Then have the dancers take partners and practice the tango march in closed position until they are thoroughly familiar with it. Observe that the proper dance walk, posture, and rhythm are being used. Students who have gained some experience should try sustaining the slow steps until the last possible moment before making the next change of weight. The quick steps are made sharply on beat. It is this contrast between the slow and quick rhythms that gives the tango its dramatic, exciting quality. The same contrast needs to be made in all tango figures. The feet remain close to the floor, but they do not shuffle.

Variations on the tango march should be explored. These include:

1. Four counts with the man moving forward, four counts with man moving backward.
2. Eight counts moving in a *small* circle, counterclockwise.
3. In semi-open position (see chapter 2), both dancers face the line of direction and move forward for eight counts; the woman uses the opposite foot to the man's but moves in the same direction.
4. Encourage the students to explore other changes of direction and position *without* changing the basic pattern of the march figure.

## The Corte

The corte (pronounced "cortay"), or stop, is a dramatic interjection that may be used on any two slow counts of any figure in the tango. For example, it may be interjected into the tango march, at counts 1 and 2. It is performed in closed position (see figure 5).

### The Corte

| Man | Count | Woman |
|---|---|---|
| Step bkwd, taking full wt on LF with left knee slightly bent & LF turned out; right leg remains straight, RF touching floor without wt | 1-& | Step fwd, taking full wt on RF with right knee slightly bent & RF turned out; left leg remains straight, toe touching floor without wt |
| Return to upright stance & step fwd, taking full wt on RF | 2-& | Return to upright stance & step bkwd, taking full wt on LF |

*Figure 5*

Counts 3–8 are the same as in the standard march figure. The turning out of the foot bearing the weight serves as a brake to prevent the dancers from dipping deeper than desired and also gives secure balance. Each dancer must support his own weight. The man must be careful not to pull his partner forward too abruptly so that she falls onto him. It requires practice and control to perform the corte smoothly.

The Tango Square (or Box)

Like other dances, the tango has a figure in which the feet make a square or box on the floor. It is done in closed position and remains in place.

### The Tango Box

| | Count | Rhythm |
|---|---|---|
| Long step fwd on LF | 1-& | S |
| Short step swd on RF | 2 | Q |
| Close LF to RF & change wt | & | Q |
| | | |
| Long step bkwd on RF | 3-& | S |
| Short step swd on LF | 4 | Q |
| Close RF to LF & change wt | & | Q |

To complete the full eight-count phrase, the figure is repeated, forming *two* box patterns.

The same figure may be developed into a turn in place using the same quarter-turns used in the primary box turn of the fox trot (see chapter 5).

The Box and Side Draw

An easy variation of the box figure uses the same steps for the first four counts, making one complete square, and then makes a variation on counts 5–8.

### The Draw

| | Count | Rhythm |
|---|---|---|
| *Long* step swd to left on LF | 5 | S |
| Slowly draw RF to arch of LF *without* changing wt | 6 | S |
| *Long* step swd to right on RF | 7 | S |
| Slowly draw LF to arch of RF *without* changing wt | 8 | S |

All box figures are danced in closed position with the woman doing the counterpart of the man's footwork. They remain in place and should be used sparingly. Generally, the tango progresses around the dancing area, and care must be taken not to impede the forward movement of other dancers.

The Diagonal March in Semi-Open Position

The diagonal march is a progressive, or traveling, figure that moves in *shallow* diagonals forward in the line of direction.

## Diagonal March in Semi-Open Position

| Man | Count | Rhythm | Woman |
|---|---|---|---|
| Step fwd on LF, turning *slightly* toward center of room | 1-& | S | Step fwd on RF, turning *slightly* toward center of room |
| Continuing shallow diag, step fwd on RF | 2-& | S | Continuing shallow diag, step fwd on LF |
| Short step fwd on LF | 3 | Q | Short step fwd on RF |
| Short step fwd on RF | & | Q | Short step fwd on LF |
| Step fwd on LF & draw partner to your left side; turn *slightly* away from center of room, still facing LOD; maintain ballroom hold, but adjust arm positions for comfort | 4-& | S | Step fwd on RF & pivot to face LOD, turning *slightly* away from center of room; maintain ballroom hold, but adjust arm positions for comfort |
| Step fwd on RF slightly away from center of room | 5-& | S | Step fwd on LF |
| Continuing outward diag, step fwd on LF | 6-& | S | Step fwd on RF |
| Short step fwd on RF | 7 | Q | Short step fwd on LF |
| Short step fwd on LF | & | Q | Short step fwd on RF |
| Step fwd on RF & draw partner into semi-open or closed position | 8-& | S | Step fwd on LF & pivot into semi-open or closed position |

## The Parade

The parade is an easy but exciting figure in which dancers progress forward, make a sudden turn, and then move backward in the line of direction. It is done in semi-open position and begins facing the line of direction.

### The Parade

| Man | Count | Rhythm | Woman |
|---|---|---|---|
| Long step fwd on LF | 1-& | S | Long step fwd on RF |
| Long step fwd on RF | 2-& | S | Long step fwd on LF |
| Long step fwd on LF | 3-& | S | Long step fwd on RF |

*continued*

| Man | Count | Rhythm | Woman |
|---|---|---|---|
| Short step on RF, making 1/4 turn CW, toward partner | 4 | Q | Short step on LF, making 1/4 turn CCW, toward partner |
| Short step on LF, making 1/4 turn CW (so that back is to LOD) & releasing right arm; partner is now on left in fully open position | & | Q | Short step on RF, making 1/4 turn CCW (so that back is to LOD) & releasing left arm from partner's shoulder; partner is now on right in fully open position |
| Long step bkwd on RF | 5-& | S | Long step bkwd on LF |
| Long step bkwd on LF | 6-& | S | Long step bkwd on RF |
| Long step bkwd on RF | 7-& | S | Long step bkwd on LF |
| Short step on LF, making 1/4 turn CCW, toward partner | 8 | Q | Short step on RF, making 1/4 turn CW, toward partner |
| Short step on RF, making 1/4 turn CCW & resuming semi-open or closed position facing LOD | & | Q | Short step on LF, making 1/4 turn CW & resuming semi-open or closed position facing LOD |

Dancers frequently repeat the parade figure to create a 16-count sequence.

## The Swingover Combination

The swingover combination progresses forward in the line of direction as the woman moves across the man, turning from side to side.

*The Swingover Combination*

| Man | Count | Rhythm | Woman |
|---|---|---|---|
| In open position, right arm behind partner's back, step fwd on LF | 1-& | S | In open position, left hand behind partner's back, step fwd on RF |
| Step fwd on RF | 2-& | S | Step fwd on LF |
| Short step fwd on LF, leading partner across in front with right arm | 3 | Q | Step across in front of partner on RF, making 1/4 turn |
| Short step fwd on RF | & | Q | Step across in front of partner on LF making 1/4 turn (so that partners are facing each other) |
| Short step fwd on LF | 4-& | S | Step across to partner's left side on RF, turning to face LOD |

| | | | |
|---|---|---|---|
| In open position, left arm behind partner's back, step fwd on RF | 5-& | S | In open position, right hand behind partner's back, step fwd on LF |
| Step fwd on LF | 6-& | S | Step fwd on RF |
| Short step fwd on RF, leading partner back across in front with left arm | 7 | Q | Step across in front of partner on LF, making 1/4 turn |
| Short step fwd on LF | & | Q | Step across in front of partner on RF, making 1/4 turn (so that partners are facing each other) |
| Short step fwd on RF | 8-& | S | Step across to partner's right side again on LF, turning to face LOD |

The dancers may repeat the swingover combination to form a 16-count sequence.

## The Dip and Turn

The dip and turn figure begins moving forward in the line of direction, then reverses, moving backward away from the line of direction and turning.

### The Dip and Turn

| Man | Count | Rhythm | Woman |
|---|---|---|---|
| In semi-open position, step fwd on LF | 1-& | S | In semi-open position, step fwd on RF |
| Step fwd on RF | 2-& | S | Step fwd on LF |
| Step fwd on LF | 3 | Q | Step fwd on RF |
| Step fwd on RF | & | Q | Step fwd on LF |
| Step fwd on LF, bending left knee into a dip or fwd corte; retain semi-open position | 4-& | S | Step fwd on RF, bending right knee into a dip or fwd corte; retain semi-open position |
| Step bkwd on RF, partially turning CW toward partner | 5-& | S | Step bkwd on LF, partially turning CCW, toward partner |
| Step toward partner on LF, completing 1/2 turn facing away from LOD | 6-& | S | Step toward partner on RF, completing 1/2 turn facing away from LOD |

*continued*

| | | | |
|---|---|---|---|
| Begin 1/2 turn in place CW, releasing partner's hands & stepping on RF | 7 | Q | Begin 1/2 turn in place CCW, releasing partner's hands & stepping on LF |
| Continue 1/2 turn in place CW, stepping on LF | & | Q | Continue 1/2 turn in place CCW, stepping on RF |
| Step on RF beside partner, resuming semi-open or closed position facing LOD | 8 | Q | Step on LF beside partner, resuming semi-open or closed position facing LOD |
| Draw LF to arch of RF, without changing wt | & | Q | Draw RF to arch of LF, without changing wt |

The dip-and-turn combination may be further enhanced by using the first 2 counts for a corte or an underarm turn.

*Underarm Turn*

| Man | Count | Rhythm | Woman |
|---|---|---|---|
| Step fwd on LF, leading partner in turn CW under your left arm while still holding her right hand | 1–& | S | Step slightly forward & to right on RF, making 1/2 turn CW under partner's arm |
| Step fwd on RF, leading partner to complete turn & ending in semi-open or closed position | 2–& | S | Step on LF completing 1/2 turn CW to end in semi-open or closed position |

The man must adjust the length of his steps to lead the woman's turn.

## The Scissors

A figure that takes its name from the crossing action of the feet is the scissors. It remains in place, with a slight side-to-side movement.

*The Scissors*

| Man | Count | Rhythm | Woman |
|---|---|---|---|
| In semi-open position, facing center of room, step fwd on LF | 1–& | S | In semi-open position, facing center of room, step fwd on RF |
| Step fwd on RF (toward center) | 2–& | S | Step fwd on LF (toward center) |
| Step on LF & turn to closed position | 3 | Q | Step on RF & turn to closed position |

| | | | |
|---|---|---|---|
| Step swd on RF, facing partner | & | Q | Step swd on LF, facing partner |
| Step across in front of yourself to right side with LF | 4–& | S | Step across in front of yourself to left side with RF |
| Step swd to right with RF | 5 | Q | Step swd to left with LF |
| Step swd on LF, facing partner | & | Q | Step swd on RF, facing partner |
| Step across in front of yourself to left side with RF | 6–& | S | Step across in front of yourself to right side with LF |
| Long step fwd on LF | 7 | Q | Long step fwd on RF |
| Step swd to right on RF | & | Q | Step swd to left on LF |
| Draw LF to arch of RF *without* changing wt | 8–& | S | Draw RF to arch of LF *without* changing wt |

On counts 3–6 of the scissors, the partners remain facing, shifting their weight from side to side with a balancing motion (see figure 6). Counts 7–8 are called the *tango close* or *tango arch,* and this combination is frequently used to end a phrase.

*Figure 6*

## PRACTICE COMBINATIONS

During initial practice sessions students should not be required to learn too many sequences at one time. It is better to work on only two or three figures until they have been thoroughly mastered; then add one or two with each subsequent lesson.

Ordinarily, the tango is not danced in any set sequence. All the figures described here are interchangeable in any order the dancers desire, as long as variety is provided. The man must use his hands and body decisively to lead his partner properly.

### Combination 1

| | |
|---|---|
| 1 tango march | 2 meas |
| 1 tango box | 2 meas |
| 1 tango march with corte | 2 meas |
| 1 tango box turn (CCW) | 2 meas |

Repeat the sequence several times.

### Combination 2

| | |
|---|---|
| 2 diagonal marches | 4 meas |
| 2 box and side draws | 4 meas |

Repeat the sequence until familiar.

### Combination 3

| | |
|---|---|
| 1 tango march with corte | 2 meas |
| 1 tango box turn (CCW) | 2 meas |
| 2 parade figures | 4 meas |

Repeat the entire sequence several times.

### Combination 4

| | |
|---|---|
| 1 tango march | 2 meas |
| 1 tango box (turning if desired) | 2 meas |
| 1 tango march in semi-open position | 2 meas |
| 1 dip and turn | 2 meas |

Repeat until all the figures flow together easily.

### Combination 5

| | |
|---|---|
| 2 swingover combinations | 4 meas |
| 1 box and draw | 2 meas |
| 1 scissors figure | 2 meas |

Repeat until the new figures are familiar.

*7*

# ᏗᎩᎾ ᏗᎷᎴᎵᎢᎪᏟᎪᏁ ᏗᎤᏚᎷᎵᎣᎪ

The dance known in the United States as the *rumba* is a composite of several dances popular in Cuba, including the *guaracha,* the *Cuban bolero,* the *Cuban son,* and the *rural rumba.* All have similar rhythms that can be traced to religious and ceremonial dances of Africa. These rhythms were remembered by the earliest black people transported unwillingly to Cuba and subjected to forced labor by the Spanish colonists. The same pulsating dance rhythms may still be found in parts of Africa, but the dances have been altered by contact with other cultures and races.

The rural rumba is a pantomimic dance originating in the rural areas. It depicts the movements of various barnyard animals in an amusing manner, and is basically an exhibition, rather than a participation, dance. Both the Cuban son and the Cuban bolero are moderate tempo dances in traditional ballroom form. The guaracha is distinguished by its fast, cheerful tempo. In styling, the American rumba closely resembles the Cuban son and the Cuban bolero.

The American rumba adaptation of the Cuban dances was first introduced in the United States in 1930. Its unique styling and unusual musical rhythms immediately captured the fancy of ballroom dance enthusiasts, and it has retained its popularity to the present time.


STYLING

The American rumba does not progress around the dancing area as the waltz and fox trot do, but rather remains in a small area with occasional traveling figures added for variety. Many positions are used including closed position, challenge position, and one-hand holds.

The earthy quality of the Afro-Cuban original is still a characteristic of the dance. In part, this is achieved by stepping *flat* on the floor while keeping the knees "soft" (partially relaxed). The pelvis of each dancer subtly swings from side to side on each count. This is achieved by relaxing the sheaf of muscles girdling the middle body enough to tilt as the body weight is transferred from one foot to the other. The action must not be initiated in the *hip* area but must be the result of the *footwork*. This shifting of the pelvis is the same action a person experiences when standing waiting for a bus, for example: the pelvis shifts from side to side as the person shifts weight from one foot to the other. In the rumba, this shifting is done to a set rhythm rather than at random.

The spinal column must also remain fluid, so that the body movement carries upward into the shoulders and neck. The head must remain controlled, but relaxed. In order to keep the knees relaxed, all steps must be *small*, not more than a few inches apart. The dancer's feet remain close to the floor but are picked up and put down; the steps must never develop into a shuffle. The desired body action is that of a flexible reed swaying in a gentle breeze.

## RHYTHM

American rumba music may be composed in either 2/4 or 4/4 time. In either case, the rhythm may be computed in counts of 4, each of equal duration. The basic footwork of the dance consists of three steps taken on the first three beats of a measure, with a hold (no step) on the fourth beat. Two measures (required for a complete pattern) can be illustrated thus:

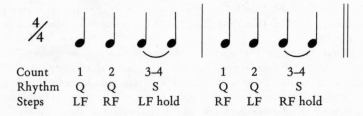

| Count  | 1  | 2  | 3-4     | 1  | 2  | 3-4     |
|--------|----|----|---------|----|----|---------|
| Rhythm | Q  | Q  | S       | Q  | Q  | S       |
| Steps  | LF | RF | LF hold | RF | LF | RF hold |

Unless students are familiar with Afro-Cuban music, they may experience some difficulty in finding the correct beat, because the African instruments in the bass section are often played in counterpoint to one another. These percussion instruments include a variety of drums, gourds, sticks, rattles, and gongs. One instrument, however, will dominate the others in bringing out the "quick, quick, slow" rhythm. The melodic line may be inspired by an old Spanish tune or the current hit from a Broadway musical. Before learning the dance steps, students should spend sufficient time learning to distinguish the dominant beat. Like most dances, the American rumba may be played in slow, moderate, or fast tempo.

## HIP MOVEMENT

To learn the pelvic sway, have the students stand with their feet not more than four or five inches apart and with their pelvic muscles relaxed. They slowly transfer their entire body weight to the left leg and foot, including the heel. The left knee must remain partly relaxed as that leg takes the weight. If the right knee and right hip are properly relaxed, the left hip will make a small movement to the left and be slightly higher than the right hip. Then the students slowly shift their body weight to the right leg and foot, noting that the reverse movement takes place. They may hold their hands on their hips to experience the sideward tilting of the pelvis. All transfers of weight need to be fluid and controlled to produce an elastic, rolling quality.

When the hip action has become familiar, dancers may add the transfer of weight in rhythm, moving *slightly* from side to side on each four counts. The verbal cue of "step, step, step, hold" is sometimes easier to follow than the more traditional "1, 2, 3, hold." Although there is no change of weight on the count of 4, *the hip movement does continue through that beat.* The dancer *anticipates* the change of weight and starts the hip moving to the opposite side in preparation for the weight shift and step on the following count of 1.

Footwork, hips, musical count, and rhythm are synchronized in this manner:

| Foot | Hip | Count | Rhythm |
|------|-----|-------|--------|
| LF | Swings left | 1 | Q |
| RF | Swings right | 2 | Q |
| LF | Swings left | 3 | S |
| Hold | Begins to swing right | 4 | |
| RF | Swings right | 1 | Q |
| LF | Swings left | 2 | Q |
| RF | Swings right | 3 | S |
| Hold | Begins to swing left | 4 | |

## FIGURES

### The Rumba Box or Square

Like many dances, the rumba contains a figure in which the feet move in a square pattern. It, like the fox-trot, has *two* box patterns, but the preferred "basic" one is similar to the secondary rhythm pattern in the fox trot, beginning with a sideward step.

With students working individually, practice the rumba box first to a count and then with music.

*The Rumba Box*

| | Count | Verbal Cue |
|---|---|---|
| Short step swd on LF | 1 | side |
| Close RF to LF & change wt | 2 | close |
| Short step fwd on LF | 3 | forward |
| Hold in place | 4 | hold |
| Short step swd on RF | 1 | side |
| Close LF to RF & change wt | 2 | close |
| Short step bkwd on RF | 3 | back |
| Hold in place | 4 | hold |

After a brief practice, permit students to take partners in closed position. The woman uses the counterpart of the man's steps. The man must not hold his partner so closely that he inhibits her freedom of movement.

The box figure may be developed into a turning one by leading with the toe turned either outward or inward on the first count and continuing to move in the direction indicated by that first step. Rumba turns are made slowly, requiring four measures or more to complete one revolution in place.

The Cuban Walk

The figure used for progressing around the dancing area is the Cuban walk. Ankles, knees, and hips must remain relaxed. Although the walk may move forward or backward, the hips continue to move from side to side, as in the box figure. Dancers must not permit their bodies to "die" on the slow count, but rather sustain the movement within their bodies. Without partners, have the students practice the steps.

*The Cuban Walk*

| | Count |
|---|---|
| Short step fwd on LF | 1 |
| Short step fwd on RF | 2 |
| Short step fwd on LF | 3 |
| Hold wt on LF (RF may touch floor beside LF without changing wt) | 4 |
| Short step fwd on RF | 1 |
| Short step fwd on LF | 2 |
| Short step fwd on RF | 3 |
| Hold wt on RF (LF may touch beside RF) | 4 |

After sufficient individual practice, partners may practice the walk in closed position with the man moving forward in the line of direction as the woman moves backward; then reverse the direction to have the man move backward. Dancers may also practice the figure in semi-open and fully open positions. The woman must step on the foot opposite that used by the man. Whenever arms are free they are permitted to move naturally without exaggerated gestures.

The rumba box and the Cuban walk may be combined in a simple exercise:

Rumba box, in place . . . . . . . . . . . . . . . . . . . . 4 meas

Cuban walk, man moving fwd . . . . . . . . . . . . . . . 4 meas

Rumba box, in place . . . . . . . . . . . . . . . . . . . . 4 meas

Cuban walk, man moving bkwd . . . . . . . . . . . . . . 4 meas

The exercise may be repeated developing the rumba box into a counterclockwise turn in place. Next, ask the students to make their own combination of the two figures, using any number of measures for each.

### The Underarm Turn

From closed position, the man marks time in place beginning with his left foot as he directs the woman under an arch formed by clasping his left and her right hand and lifting the hands and arms upward (see figure 7). The woman begins

*Figure 7*

with her right foot, using the Cuban walk, to make a small, slow turn in place. Four measures or more should be taken to make a full revolution and end facing the man again.

Likewise, the man may turn under the arch while the woman marks time in place.

## The Wheel Turn

A wheel turn is one in which partners turn around an imaginary axis common to both. Various hand positions may be used.

In a *one-hand hold,* the dancers' hands make the axis around which they revolve (see figure 8). Standing in a line side by side but facing in opposite directions, the dancers join inside hands (the woman's right in the man's right hand when right sides are adjacent; left hands joined when left sides are adjacent). Arms are held with elbows slightly bent to bring partners close together. Using a series of Cuban walk figures, the dancers move in a small clockwise circle for as long as desired. To change to a counterclockwise circle, the dancers release hands and turn slowly toward one another, still using Cuban walk steps, until their left sides are adjacent and left hands are joined. The free hands are relaxed and move naturally with the rhythm of the dancers' bodies.

*Figure 8*

The same turn may be made with both hands joined in a *cross-hand, or skating, position.* The man's right hand should hold the woman's right; his left hand her left. On making the change of direction, the dancers do not release hands, but simply turn slowly in place to bring their opposite sides adjacent. With this hand hold, dancers will be almost shoulder to shoulder, each moving directly forward in the direction he or she is facing (except when changing directions).

The wheel turn may also be done in *closed position.* The man steps to his left to bring the right side of his body adjacent to the woman's right side. Using Cuban walk steps, they turn in a clockwise circle for the desired number of measures. Then, continuing to use the Cuban walk, partners turn in place to bring their left sides adjacent and turn in a counterclockwise circle. The closed position is retained throughout, but slightly modified to allow for comfort.

All wheel turns may also be performed moving *backward,* as an interesting variation.

### The Rumba Dos-a-Dos

An easy figure popular with young dancers is the rumba dos-a-dos. It is similar to one used in American square dancing, but uses the Cuban walk.

Partners face each other and advance to pass right shoulders. Without turning around, each moves sideward to pass back-to-back. Then, moving backward to pass left shoulders, they return to their original places. Any number of measures may be used to complete the figure.

In the rumba, when fast-tempo music is used, the footwork must be *proportionately smaller.* A common error made by beginning dancers is to increase the size of the steps with a faster tempo.

### PRACTICE COMBINATIONS

A rumba dancer need not know a vast number of elaborate figures, but he must be able to combine the ones he knows with deftness and imagination.

As each new figure is taught, it should be combined with one or two other figures to achieve a smooth blending without loss of the characteristic rhythm and styling. A few suggestions are listed below.

### Combination 1

| | |
|---|---|
| 1 complete rumba box | 4 meas |
| 8 Cuban walk steps in semi-open position (ending to face partner) | 8 meas |
| 1 underarm turn, woman turning | 4 meas |
| 1 underarm turn, man turning | 4 meas |

Repeat the sequence from the beginning.

Combination 2

8 Cuban walk steps in fully open position   . . . . . . . . . 8 meas
1 CW wheel turn, right hands joined   . . . . . . . . . . . 4 meas
1 CCW wheel turn, left hands joined   . . . . . . . . . . . 4 meas
2 rumba box figures   . . . . . . . . . . . . . . . . . 8 meas
Repeat all from the beginning.

Combination 3

8 Cuban walk steps in closed position (man facing LOD)   . . . . . 8 meas
1 rumba box   . . . . . . . . . . . . . . . . . . . . 4 meas
1underarm turn, woman turning   . . . . . . . . . . . . . 4 meas
1dos-a-dos   . . . . . . . . . . . . . . . as many meas as required
Repeat from the beginning.

# 8

# Swing

The 1930s were years of financial depression and hardship, yet they were also years during which ballroom dance reached one of its highest peaks of popularity and finesse in the United States. Every community, no matter how small, possessed a public dance pavilion. Larger cities frequently filled several dance palaces to capacity every night. Major hotels expanded their dining rooms to allow an area for ballroom dancing.

It was during this era that dance orchestras changed from small groups playing improvizational jazz to sophisticated big bands frequently of thirty to forty highly trained musicians. Each selection was meticulously prepared by a musical arranger to create the most agreeable harmonics from the large ensemble of instruments at his command. By 1935, more than 300 dance orchestras were in existence. Even the most renowned made extended tours doing one-night stands in small rural communities, playing for a week or two at state and county fairs, and fulfilling long commitments in large cities.

Competition among the bands was strong, and many conductors and arrangers experimented with new musical sounds or rhythms that would uniquely identify their own groups. Some bands were distinguished for their sweetly sentimental fox-trots and waltzes, while others adhered to the older styles, mainly either New Orleans jazz or Chicago-style jazz developed in the 1920s. Benny Goodman is the band leader credited with developing the rhythm eventually known as *swing*. Goodman, who was a virtuoso of both classical and popular music, reverted to the musical styling used by many of the black musicians in New York's Harlem and rural areas of the Deep South. Like the ragtime of earlier years, this music shifted the accent from the first count to the second, producing a "swinging" rhythm. Goodman's success with the new sound prompted a number of other groups to follow. Wherever these bands played, they attracted an enormous following of young people whose exuberance overflowed in a manner that was to be repeated by the same age group years later at the rock festivals of the 1960s.

The fox-trot—that perpetual, versatile standby of generations of ballroom dancers—did not fit the swinging, bounding rhythm of the new music. It did not take long for suitable dances to come into being. The *lindy hop*, a novelty dance named for Charles Lindbergh's solo flight across the Atlantic in 1927, was revived to fit the new music in the New York area. Students of the ivy league colleges developed an exaggerated hopping dance in which their feet swung backward and forward like pendulums, and called it *the shag*. Out of Harlem came an exhibition dance involving exuberant acrobatics and perfectly coordinated team-work; to a base of elaborate, rhythmic footwork were added spectacular jumps and lifts. A newspaper columnist of the era remarked that the dance resembled a bunch of "jittery bugs," and the name *jitterbug* thereafter identified that particular dance style.

The lindy hop, shag, jitterbug, and similar dances appealed strongly to teen-age dancers, who created their own versions. Each neighborhood and every city had its methods of dancing to swing music. For many months, dance teacher organizations ignored the new style of dancing. But the public demand became so great, they could not overlook it. In time, dance organizations standardized a version to a six-beat count, which was adopted by dancers throughout the United States. The new form of the dance acquired the name *swing* from the term applied to the music.

Other dances of the period using swing rhythm included the *big apple, trucking,* and *be-bop*. In the 1940s, GIs carried swing music and dances to the battlefronts of World War II, where they were quickly adopted by youthful natives.

## STYLING

The acrobatic quality that distinguished the early jitterbug contributed close cooperation and coordinated timing to six-beat swing. The basic footwork is repetitious and can be exceptionally dull without the proper interaction between partners. While different hand positions may be used, both dancers need to maintain a certain degree of tension in their arms to create an elastic, springlike quality. Swing resembles two acrobats working together, each ever alert to catch the other. The dancers use their bodies in a manner unique to this dance. The entire upper torso swings either forward and backward or from side to side, with a sense of resistance like that encountered while moving in water.

The woman does not perform the exact counterpart of the man's steps. Although she uses the opposite foot, she steps forward at the *same time* he moves forward, and backward as he steps backward. The footwork remains small and springy in quality, although most steps are made on either the flat or the ball of the foot. Swing is a "spot" dance—the dancers remain in one area but do figures that move the partners around each other.

Swing may be performed in semi-open position, in which case it generally moves from side to side. Most young people prefer the freedom of the face-to-face position (see figure 9) with either one or both hands joined. In this position the footwork moves generally forward and backward toward and away from one's partner. For the sake of simplicity, this position is assumed in the written descriptions.

*Figure 9*

RHYTHM

The complete dance phrase in swing requires six beats of music. Swing music is composed in both 2/4 and 4/4 time, but in either case a definite two-beat rhythm should be dominant. In 4/4 time, the dance pattern requires 1½ measures of music; in 2/4 time, it uses 3 measures.

The names of the foundation figures of swing were borrowed from the older lindy hop; they are the *single lindy*, the *double lindy*, and the *triple lindy*.

Although there are subtle variations among the three patterns, each requires only six beats of music.

A three-measure sequence of 2/4 music used with the single lindy is depicted:

| Count | 1 | 2 | 3 | 4 | 5 | 6 |
|---|---|---|---|---|---|---|
| Rhythm | S | | S | | Q | Q |
| Man's Steps | LF | hold | RF | hold | LF | RF |
| Woman's Steps | RF | hold | LF | hold | RF | LF |

Contrary to most dances, the pattern does not alternate. The man always begins the six-count sequence with his *left* foot; the woman begins with her *right* foot.

It is sometimes easier to count 1-2, 1-2, 1-2. The six-count phrasing is not written into the music; therefore individual couples may begin on *any* count of 1.

## FIGURES

### The Single Lindy

For initial practice, separate men and women. After a brief practice with the men, proceed to teach the women. In the lindy the women do not do the counterpart of the men's footwork because both step *forward* on the count of 1.

Because the dance phrase is short, both footwork and styling may be emphasized at the same time. All footwork must be compact. A common fault is to step too far backward on the left foot.

### *The Single Lindy*

| Man | Count | Rhythm | Woman |
|---|---|---|---|
| Short step fwd on flat of LF, bending left knee & pushing upper torso fwd with resistance | 1 | S | Short step fwd on flat of RF, bending right knee & pushing upper torso fwd with resistance |
| Hold LF in place without changing wt | 2 | | Hold RF in place without changing wt |
| Short step bkwd on flat of RF, pulling torso bkwd with resistance & keeping right knee "soft" | 3 | S | Short step bkwd on flat of LF |

| | | |
|---|---|---|
| Hold RF in place without changing wt | 4 | Hold LF in place without changing wt |
| Short step bkwd on LF, toe turned out & trunk of body slightly twisted to left | 5 | Q |
| Step in place on RF, turning body to face fwd | 6 | Q |

Short step bkwd on RF, toe turned out & trunk of body slightly twisted to right

Step in place on LF, turning body to face fwd

Because it is contrary to the rules of most standard dances, it must be clearly delineated that in swing the woman steps forward as the man steps forward. For both men and women, the directional cue, "Forward, hold, back, hold, step, step," will assist dancers with the footwork.

After brief practice sessions to a verbal count and to recorded music, permit students to take partners and practice together. This introduces a new element: proper use of the hands and arms. It is as important as the correct footwork and body placement.

For the beginning practice period, partners extend arms straight across to join both hands. The man holds his hands palm upward with fingers turning back toward himself; the woman holds her hands with palms downward and fingers turned back toward herself. The woman hooks her fingers over those of the man; he tightens his grasp to create a secure grip.

Arms of both dancers are bent at the elbow at an approximate right angle. Elbows remain close to the dancer's own body. *Both* men and women retain a controlled amount of tension in arms and elbows to create a springlike bond between them. When correctly used, the arms also serve as shock absorbers to prevent the dancers' bodies from whipping about dangerously.

Have the students combine footwork and body action, with the following arm actions.

### The Single Lindy

| Arm Movements | Count | Rhythm |
|---|---|---|
| Dancers pull together | 1–2 | S |
| Dancers push apart to a normal standing position | 3–4 | S |
| Dancers push slightly backward beyond normal standing position | 5 | Q |
| Dancers pull forward and together to standing position | 6 | Q |

The rhythm, body placement, and use of hands in all other swing figures are based on those of the single lindy; this figure should be thoroughly understood before dancers progress to other patterns.

The single lindy may also turn in place. A turn is initiated by turning the toe of the leading foot either inward or outward on count 1. The body continues to fol· ·/ the direction indicated for as long as the leader desires. Turns may be ma··  counterclockwise or clockwise, with both dancers turning around an im· ·nary axis. Turns should progress by slow degrees, never rapidly, in the d· ·ed direction.

## The Double Lindy

·· ·e double lindy uses the same rhythm, styling, and hand movements as the ·gle lindy. The principal difference is that the count of 2, which was held in ·e single lindy, is filled in by one of several different methods. In the following ·ree examples, both dancers must step forward toward their partners, men ·eginning with the left foot, women with the right foot.

### Double Lindy 1

|  | Counts |
|---|---|
| "Dig" ball of foot into floor as you step fwd | 1 |
| Bring *heel* of same foot down hard on floor | 2 |
| Step bkwd, digging ball of opposite foot into floor | 3 |
| Bring *heel* of same foot down hard on floor | 4 |
| Same steps as single lindy | 5–6 |

### Double Lindy 2

|  | Counts |
|---|---|
| Step fwd on flat foot | 1 |
| *Tap* free foot beside standing foot (using flat foot, toe, or heel) | 2 |
| Step bkwd on flat foot | 3 |
| *Tap* free foot beside standing foot | 4 |
| Same as single lindy | 5–6 |

### Double Lindy 3

|  | Counts |
|---|---|
| Swing leg fwd & *tap* foot to floor | 1 |
| Step *in place* on same foot | 2 |
| Swing opposite leg bkwd & *tap* foot to floor | 3 |
| Step *in place* on same foot | 4 |
| Same as single lindy | 5–6 |

Although students should practice all three versions, they will ultimately select the version that is most comfortable for their own use. Because the basic rhythm is the same in *all* figures of swing, it is not mandatory for partners to use identical footwork. One partner may be using the single lindy while the other may be using any version of the double lindy.

The double lindy may also be directed to turn in place. Turns should be practiced both clockwise and counterclockwise.

As dancers develop skill and coordination, they may change from the two-hand hold to a one-hand hold. Any combination may be used: right hands joined, left hands joined, left in right, or right in left. The timing of changes in hand positions must be coordinated to maintain the necessary tension in the arms. In most cases it is best to make the hand change on the count of 1, as dancers are moving forward toward one another.

## The Triple Lindy

The triple lindy uses the same basic six counts as the single lindy and double lindy figures. The two slow counts of the rhythm are replaced by triplets. A triplet consists of *three* changes of weight made to the two beats of music. All steps are short and fast. For initial practice of the triple lindy, slow-tempo music should be used. Men begin with the *left* foot, women with the *right*.

### The Triple Lindy

|  | Counts |
| --- | --- |
| Short step fwd on ball of foot | 1 |
| Close free foot to standing foot & change wt | & |
| Short step fwd on ball of foot | 2–& |
| Short step bkwd on ball of foot | 3 |
| Close free foot to standing foot & change wt | & |
| Short step bkwd on ball of foot | 4–& |
| Same as single lindy | 5–6 |

## The Walkaround

The walkaround is a complete change from the single, double, and triple lindy. It affords an interesting variation without departing from the spirit of swing.

Numerous positions may be used with the walkaround, but the one generally favored by beginning dancers is a side-by-side position, similar to the "swing-your-partner" position used in American square dancing. From one of the lindy figures, the man quickly steps forward and pivots, to bring his right hip adjacent to that of his partner. Any logical hand positions may be used. The dancers then revolve in place, using a series of short, jabbing steps to each beat of the music.

The transition must be made without pausing or losing the beat. To return to one of the lindy figures, an *even* number of steps—six, eight, or ten—must be used for the walkaround.

As a practice sequence, have the students alternate one single lindy figure with eight steps of the walkaround. All transitions must be made without hesitation or loss of rhythm.

Encourage students to explore various positions and hand holds for use with the walkaround. Generally, dancers pull away from one another with their shoulders, thus keeping their feet close together.

## The Underarm Crossover

Advanced swing dancers use a variety of turning figures, but for beginners the underarm crossover is effective and easy. Initially, the basic footwork of the single lindy figure should be used. With more experience, the double or triple lindy figures may be substituted.

The man holds the woman's right hand in his right hand and raises their arms to make an arch. In effect, both dancers move toward and around each other to exchange places on counts 1–4. At the same time, the man leads his partner *under* the arch formed by their arms so that she makes a complete turn to her right (clockwise). Counts 5 and 6 are the same as in the basic figure. In exchanging places, partners need to remain close together. A quick adjustment of the hand clasp must be made to facilitate the turn.

After the technique of the underarm turn has been practiced to a slow tempo, have the students alternate the figure with a single lindy performed in place. The combination of the two figures will prevent the dancers from becoming dizzy.

When dancers have gained experience, the underarm turn may be made on the opposite side. The footwork remains the same but hand positions must be changed so that the man holds the woman's left hand in his left hand.

## The Open Breakaway Variation

As dancers gain experience in swing, the open breakaway figure may be added to the basic footwork. For simplicity, have dancers begin with the single lindy footwork; later the double or triple lindy may be used instead.

With a two-hand hold straight across, the dancers do the single lindy steps for counts 1–4. On count 5, the man pushes the woman backward with his *left* hand, causing her to step farther than she normally would. On the same count, he releases his left hand from her right, and he steps backward with his left foot. Momentarily, the partners are in an open line, side by side. Their free arms open gracefully outward. On count 6, the man quickly draws his partner toward him, using his right hand, which has kept hold of her left hand.

With practice, the hand action may be reversed to open to the opposite side. (The footwork remains the same.)

## PRACTICE COMBINATIONS

Most young dancers prefer the freedom of movement allowed by the challenge position, with their choice of hand holds. However, swing should also be practiced in closed position. The restraint of this position requires some adjustments in the steps. For example, the footwork must become more sideward than forward and backward (see figure 10).

*Figure 10*

Students should be encouraged to combine all figures, patterns, and positions into free, creative, and interesting sequences. Memorized sequences tend to be danced in a lethargic manner that does not fit the lively spirit of swing. The following combinations are listed as a practice device to assure a thorough progression and combination of figures. The term *sequence* is used in place of measures. It refers to the regular six-count footwork required for the lindy figures. Initially, all patterns will begin with the two-hand hold.

### Combination 1

Single lindy . . . . . . . . . . . . . . . . . . . . . . . 4 sequences

Single lindy, turning in place with partner . . . . . . . . . 4 sequences

Repeat several times.

Combination 2

> Double lindy (any version) . . . . . . . . . . . . . 4 sequences
> Double lindy, turning in place with partner . . . . . . . . 4 sequences
> Repeat several times.

Combination 3

> Single lindy . . . . . . . . . . . . . . . . . . 1 sequence
> Underarm crossover . . . . . . . . . . . . . . . 1 sequence
> Repeat until the crossover is achieved without losing the rhythm.

Combination 4

> Double lindy . . . . . . . . . . . . . . . . . . 4 sequences
> Walkaround (turning in small circle) . . . . . . . . . . . 8 counts
> Repeat until the transition is made without hesitation.

Combination 5

> Single lindy . . . . . . . . . . . . . . . . . . 1 sequence
> Open breakaway . . . . . . . . . . . . . . . . 1 sequence
> Repeat until the opening and closing of the breakaway is thoroughly
> understood. Then try to alternate the side to which the breakaway opens.

Combination 6

> Repeat all the above practice sequences substituting triple lindy footwork for
> the single or double lindy.

# 9

# The Samba

Since the days when Brazil was a colony of Portugal, the Lenten season preceding Easter has been celebrated with a series of holiday parades, satirical pantomimes, dancing in the open streets, and general merrymaking. A popular and important feature of the celebrations has always been the original and imaginative songs and dances by the black Brazilians of African descent. One of the original dances was the batuque, danced to pulsating African rhythms played on a variety of drums, rattles, and gongs. As the paraders moved along the streets with jaunty, body-swinging, rhythmic movements, a leader would occasionally shout, "Semba!" This was a command to stop and perform a series of freely improvised dances. In time, the command "Semba!" became the identifying name of the dance to the spectators. Eventually the spelling and pronunciation was altered to samba.

During the late 1920s and early 1930s, the American fox trot dominated the social dance scene in the upper-class ballrooms of Brazil. Innovative dancers, however, successfully modified their native carnival dance to a more restricted closed-position dance—at that time considered the only correct position for social dances. Saucy, bouncy, and exuberant, the samba wended its way from Brazil to the ballrooms of the United States in 1939. The ballroom version was slow to reach popularity in the United States and Europe, because musicians in those countries did not understand the complex percussion rhythms the Brazilians had inherited from black African culture.

## STYLING

The samba is characterized by a pendular swing of the dancers' bodies. The movement is smooth and controlled but still exudes the joy and enthusiasm typical of the dance. Like other dances of African influence, it uses the pelvic area as an important factor in the styling. The pelvis serves as a "hinge" separating the upper body from the legs. The objective is to have the legs and feet swing forward and backward in a greater arc than that of the upper body. This is accomplished by a slight contraction and release of the pelvic muscles. The muscles are contracted as the feet and legs move forward, tilting the pelvis forward from the base of the spine. The muscles are then relaxed as the feet and legs move backward, permitting a slight backward tilt of the pelvis. The movement must be initiated from the feet, not from the pelvic region.

The feet use a slightly springing action, which is carried throughout the body in a smoothly controlled manner. It is aided by keeping knees and ankles relaxed and pliable.

Whenever arms and hands are free they are permitted to move in a natural manner to complement the undulating body motion. Exaggerated, artificial arm positions are no longer considered to be in good taste in the samba.

The samba is similar to the rumba in that it does not progress around the room as the fox trot and waltz do. It remains in a relatively limited area, while the dancers perform free patterns of movement with, or around, their partners. The samba uses many dance positions, changing from one to another smoothly, without hesitation or loss of rhythm.

## RHYTHM

The samba has a distinct rhythm that readily suggests the lilting, swaying movements of the dance. Once this rhythm becomes familiar, the dancer will not easily confuse it with any other. Samba music is composed in 2/4 time. A two-measure dance phrase may be illustrated thus:

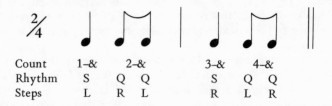

| Count | 1–& | 2–& | | 3–& | 4–& |
|-------|-----|-----|---|-----|-----|
| Rhythm | S | Q  Q | | S | Q  Q |
| Steps | L | R  L | | R | L  R |

*Three* changes of weight are made for each *two* beats of music, and the footwork alternates with each measure. Before learning the footwork, students must become thoroughly familiar with the music by listening to several selections. Once the "slow, quick, quick" rhythm is recognized, the music will greatly facilitate the correct footwork.

## FIGURES

### The Pendulum (or Bell Figure)

Unlike most dances, the samba has *two* basic figures. Both use the same rhythm but they require different footwork and serve different purposes. The pendulum or bell figure may be taught first.

### The Pendulum

|  | Count | Rhythm |
|---|---|---|
| Step fwd on flat of LF | 1–& | S |
| Step fwd beside LF on ball of RF | 2 | Q |
| Step in place beside RF on flat of LF | & | Q |
| Step bkwd on flat of RF | 3–& | S |
| Step bkwd beside RF on ball of LF | 4 | Q |
| Step in place beside LF on flat of RF | & | Q |

The dancers' feet remain close to the floor to produce a gliding rather than a prancing motion. As the name pendulum suggests, the feet swing forward and backward in a greater arc than the head and shoulders. As previously stated, the pelvic area serves as an imaginary hinge that permits the pendular action to take place. As the feet move forward, the pelvic area is slightly contracted, and the body tilts backward a bit; as the feet move backward, the pelvic muscles are released, and the body tilts forward a bit. Both feet remain closely parallel, toes pointing forward during the forward and backward steps.

The proper footwork will produce a slight bounce-bounce-bounce movement, which should be permitted to carry upward throughout the body, but in a controlled, relaxed manner. Whenever hands and arms are free, they follow the body rhythm in a normal way.

Students should practice the pendulum figure without partners until they can coordinate body action and footwork. Then they may dance together in closed position, the woman using the counterpart of the man's footwork.

The pendulum figure does not travel. It may turn in place, however, in either direction. The turn is initiated by leading with the toe pointed in the direction of the turn on the count of 1. Feet must remain close together as the turn is made.

### The Samba Walk

The second basic figure is the samba walk. As the name suggests, it is used for traveling. The rhythm and styling are the same as in the pendulum figure but the footwork is different. The samba walk moves only *forward* in the line of direction; it is never used in a closed or face-to-face position. In other words, neither men or women use the figure to move backward.

The samba walk employs the same contract-and-release action in the pelvic area as the pendulum figure. The steps are small, feet remaining close to the floor. For initial practice, both men and women should perform without partners.

### Samba Walk

|  | Count | Rhythm |
|---|---|---|
| Step fwd on flat of LF, knee relaxed; (RF remains in place, without wt on it) | 1-& | S |
| Step bkwd on ball of RF | 2 | Q |
| Move LF slightly bkwd to step flat about halfway between the first two changes of wt | & | Q |
| Step fwd on flat of RF, knee relaxed | 3-& | S |
| Step bkwd (in place) on ball of LF | 4 | Q |
| Step halfway bkwd on flat of RF | & | Q |

After the students become familiar with the samba walk, permit them to take partners. Both face in the same direction, the woman on the man's right, in open position (see figure 3 at page 17). The man begins with his left foot and the woman with her right. Couples may practice the samba walk moving around the room. The rate of progress is slow; the usual beginner's error is to attempt to move too rapidly, taking steps that are too long. Free arms and hands move naturally.

After a brief practice of the samba walk using correct rhythm and styling, couples may practice a simple combination alternating six measures each of the pendulum figure and the samba walk. The man must anticipate the proper timing to lead his partner from one position to the other. The transition must be made without losing rhythm and styling. When this has been accomplished, dancers may try using any number of measures for each of the two figures. The choice of measures should be the responsibility of the leader alone. He must indicate the changes by the use of his hands and body, never by a verbal command.

## Individual Circles

Partners may travel individually in small circles, first *away* from each other and then, as they complete their circles, back toward their partners. Generally, the man turns to his left (counterclockwise), while the woman turns to her right (clockwise). The footwork is the samba walk. Arms move freely to the body movement; artificial positions, which were erroneously applied to the samba when it was first introduced in the United States, have been considered obsolete for many years. The individual circles should not be too large; six or eight measures are enough for practical purposes.

For an easy practice combination, have the dancers alternate six measures of pendulum with six of individual circles.

### The Wheel Turn

Wheel turns are figures that revolve around an imaginary central axis. Various hand positions may be used, but for beginners the most simple is one in which the man and woman join their right hands (see figure 8 at page 64). The dancers face in opposite directions as they travel forward in a small clockwise circle, using the samba walk. To change the line of direction to a counterclockwise circle, the dancers turn inward toward one another, using the samba walk. They join left hands and continue to progress in the new direction. The transition must be made smoothly without losing the rhythm.

As an easy practice combination, have the students circle clockwise with right hands joined for five measures. On the sixth measure they release hands and turn inward to change the direction of the circle. Then they move in a counter-clockwise direction for five measures, and change again on the sixth. The man cues the change of direction by gently pushing backward on the woman's hand before releasing it. The free arms move naturally as a part of the dance; wooden arms are to be avoided.

If desired, the dancers may first turn counterclockwise with left hands joined. They should alternate a series of six-measure circles until the transitions, styling, and rhythm have become comfortable and are thoroughly understood.

### Basic Figure Combinations

All the samba figures that have been learned may be combined into the following practice sequence.

| | |
|---|---:|
| 3 pendulum figures fwd (closed position) . . . . . . . . . . . | 6 meas |
| 3 samba walks fwd (semi-open position) . . . . . . . . . . | 6 meas |
| 3 pendulum figures fwd (closed position) . . . . . . . . . . | 6 meas |
| 1 individual circle (man CCW, woman CW) . . . . . . . . . | 6 meas |
| 1 wheel turn CW (right hands joined) . . . . . . . . . . . | 6 meas |
| 1wheel turn CCW (left hands joined) . . . . . . . . . . . | 6 meas |

Throughout *all* samba figures, partners use opposite feet: when the man's weight is on his left foot, the woman's should be on her right foot and vice versa.

Repeat the sequence several times until the dancers make all transitions involving hand changes, positions, and footwork in a smooth, relaxed manner. The men must learn to anticipate the changes to give the proper cue to their partners. Carefully observe that the men are leading, not the women.

Next have the students combine the same figures in any order, using varying numbers of measures for each. All figures and transitions are to be initiated and led by the man. He must strive to be imaginative and spontaneous, rather than following a memorized sequence.

Encourage dancers to use other positions for the same basic figures. For example, they may use an open position with both hands free for the samba walk; wheel turns may be made without joining hands; or in the pendulum figure the man may place both hands on the woman's waist while she places her hands on his upper arms.

As dancers become proficient in the basic figures of the samba, they will enjoy learning a few of the more advanced steps.

## The Side Pendulum

The pendulum figure may also move from side to side. Instead of tilting forward and back, the pelvis tilts from side to side, but this motion must be controlled to avoid a twisting action. For initial practice, dancers should do the step individually.

*The Side Pendulum*

|  | Count | Rhythm |
|---|---|---|
| Short step swd on flat of LF | 1–& | S |
| Step behind LF on toe of RF | 2 | Q |
| Step in place on flat of LF | & | Q |
| Short step swd on flat of RF | 3–& | S |
| Step behind LF on toe of RF | 4 | Q |
| Step in place on flat of LF | & | Q |

Care must be taken not to step too far backward on the counts 2 and 4.

In closed position, the woman does the counterpart of the man's steps; as he steps to the left onto his left foot, she steps to her right onto her right foot.

After dancers have gained sufficient practice in the side pendulum, a simple combination may be used, such as the following:

2 pendulum figures (fwd & bkwd) . . . . . . . . . . . . 4 meas
2 side pendulums . . . . . . . . . . . . . . . . . . . 4 meas
2 samba walks (semi-open position) . . . . . . . . . . 4 meas
2 side pendulums . . . . . . . . . . . . . . . . . . . 4 meas

Repeat the sequence until the dancers understand and correctly perform all transitions.

The Copacabana Walk

The Copacabana walk (also called the Copa walk) is an easy variation on the samba walk done in slightly more exaggerated style. Because this figure requires freedom of movement, it should be danced in a variation of the fully open position with inside hands joined (see figure 11). A no-contact position may also be used, in which dancers move side by side. The free arms and hands move slightly more vigorously than in most figures.

*Figure 11*

Basically, the Copacabana walk is like the samba walk except that the foot that steps forward on the count of 1 is turned *outward*. If the pelvic region is properly relaxed this will cause the hips to swing in the opposite direction, thus causing the dancers to turn away and then toward each other with each two beats of the music.

*The Copacabana Walk*

|  | Count | Rhythm |
|---|---|---|
| Step fwd on flat of LF, turning foot outward to left (hips swing to right) | 1-& | S |

*continued*

| | | |
|---|---|---|
| Step bkwd on ball of RF | 2 | Q |
| Step slightly bkwd on flat of LF about halfway between first two changes of wt | & | Q |
| Step fwd on flat of RF, turning foot outward to right (hips swing to left) | 3–& | S |
| Step bkwd on toe of LF | 4 | Q |
| Step slightly bkwd on flat of RF halfway between first two changes of wt | & | Q |

Men and women use opposite feet but move forward and backward at the same times. Relaxation is the secret of performing the Copacabana walk with style and vitality. This figure may be used instead of the samba walk to travel and to make individual circles. The twisting motion in the hips must come as the result of the footwork, not by force.

## The Samba Box or Square

Because the samba box figure develops a counter motion in the upper part of the body that is difficult for a beginner to control, it should be reserved for dancers who have gained a degree of proficiency.

This figure resembles the waltz square, but it is performed in the "slow, quick, quick" rhythm of the samba. If the pelvic area is properly relaxed, the upper part of the body will develop a motion counter to that of the legs and feet. This motion should not be forced. The samba box is done in closed position.

### The Samba Box

| Man | Count | Rhythm | Woman |
|---|---|---|---|
| Step fwd on flat of LF | 1–& | S | Step bkwd on flat of RF |
| Short step swd on ball of RF | 2 | Q | Short step swd on ball of LF |
| Close LF to RF, stepping on flat of LF | & | Q | Close RF to LF, stepping on flat of RF |
| Step bkwd on flat of RF | 3–& | S | Step fwd on flat of LF |
| Short step swd on ball of LF | 4 | Q | Short step swd on ball of RF |
| Close RF to LF, stepping on flat of RF | & | Q | Close LF to RF, stepping on flat of LF |

Like all box figures, the samba box may also turn in place. The turning technique is the same as that used in the waltz or fox trot box. Ankles, knees, and pelvic area must remain pliable.

## PRACTICE COMBINATIONS

### Combination 1

Sometimes one partner dances the basic pendulum figure while the other does the samba walk. For example, beginning in fully open position, side by side, with inside hands joined, the man does the pendulum figure in place as he leads the woman around himself in a large circle. She does the samba walk (or Copacabana walk) to progress *slowly* around him. The number of measures required to complete the circle varies.

### Combination 2

| | |
|---|---|
| 2 side pendulums (closed position) | 4 meas |
| 2 pendulums fwd & bkwd (closed position) | 4 meas |
| 2 side pendulums (closed position) | 4 meas |
| 2 pendulums (closed position) | 4 meas |
| 1 individual circle (man CCW, woman CW) | 8 meas |
| 2 samba box steps (closed position) | 8 meas |
| 4 samba walks (semi-open position) | 8 meas |

Repeat from the beginning.

### Combination 3

| | |
|---|---|
| 4 Copacabana walks | 8 meas |
| 4 pendulums turning in place (closed position) | 8 meas |
| 1 wheel turn CW (right shoulders adjacent, hands *not* joined) | 8 meas |
| 1 wheel turn CCW (left shoulders adjacent, hands *not* joined) | 8 meas |
| 6 pendulums in place by man, while woman makes CCW circle around him with samba walk | 12 meas |

Repeat from the beginning.

# 10

# The Cha-Cha

In the late 1940s, Havana, Cuba, was one of the most popular resorts for North Americans, especially those residing along the east coast. The most famous American dance bands as well as the many outstanding Latin bands native to Cuba played at the city's casinos. Some of these orchestras tried combining the American jazz beat with the Cuban rumba rhythm. The result was a new rhythm called the mambo, a term freely borrowed from African voodoo religion, in which the cult priestesses are honored with this name.

A dance was developed to the new mambo rhythm, danced to the off beat rather than the traditional downbeat. For this reason, the dance was popular mainly with dancers thoroughly familiar with complex Afro-Cuban music. However, among the many figures of the mambo was one called the *chatch,* which involved three quick changes of weight preceded by two slow steps. By the early 1950s, this figure had developed into a new dance comprised of many simple variations on the basic footwork. The dance acquired the name cha-cha; its characteristic three-step change of weight carried the identifying verbal definition, "cha, cha, cha."

## STYLING

The cha-cha inherited much of its styling from its parent dances, the rumba and the mambo. It is a dance that remains in place and may be danced in closed position, challenge position, or a combination of both. Like most Latin dances, it is done with the feet remaining close to the floor. The dancers' hips are relaxed to allow free movement in the pelvic section. The upper body shifts over the supporting foot, as steps are taken forward, backward or sideward. Feet are placed flat on the floor and knees are kept relaxed. When hands and arms are free, they move expressively in natural rhythm with the body.

In closed position, the dance is more restricted in movement, and the woman performs the counterpart of the man's steps. When challenge position is used, each dancer is free to choose his own figures as long as they follow the common rhythm. Dancers revolve around one another, and exchange places back and forth.

## RHYTHM

Cha-cha music is composed in 4/4 time. There are four beats to the measure, but the third beat is divided into two eighth notes. The resulting rhythm is cued, "Slow, slow, quick, quick, slow."

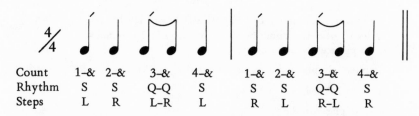

| Count | 1-& | 2-& | 3-& | 4-& | 1-& | 2-& | 3-& | 4-& |
|---|---|---|---|---|---|---|---|---|
| Rhythm | S | S | Q-Q | S | S | S | Q-Q | S |
| Steps | L | R | L-R | L | R | L | R-L | R |

The cha-cha is danced "on the beat;" that is, the footwork must coincide with the basic rhythm. An easy verbal count is, "Step, step, cha, cha, cha." Students must learn to hear the rhythm before attempting the dance.

As an exercise to learn the steps of the cha-cha in rhythm, have the students mark time in place with both men and women using the same footwork without partners.

| Steps | Count | Rhythm | Verbal Cue |
|---|---|---|---|
| Step in place on LF | 1-& | S | step |
| Step in place on RF | 2-& | S | step |
| Step in place on LF | 3 | Q | cha |
| Step in place on RF | & | Q | cha |
| Step in place on LF | 4-& | S | cha |

Then have them reverse the footwork to begin with the right foot on count 1. Note that there are five changes of weight to each measure of music, and the footwork alternates with each measure. Although some advanced figures differ, the many simpler figures of the cha-cha are based on this five change pattern. It should be repeated until the students are thoroughly familiar with it. When music is used, make certain that the footwork corresponds to the slow, slow, quick, quick, slow rhythm in the musical base. Do not permit the students to begin the "cha, cha, cha" steps on the slow counts. When the footwork and the rhythm have been correctly coordinated, it is time to progress to the cha-cha basic figure and to add the typical styling.

## FIGURES

### The Cha-Cha Basic

The cha-cha basic employs a rocking step, forward and backward, that is used in the majority of other cha-cha figures. Both men and women should practice the same footwork, initially. The *forward* rock is done first.

#### The Cha-Cha Basic (Forward)

|  | Count | Rhythm |
|---|---|---|
| Short step fwd, on ball of LF, with left knee slightly bent; let wt of entire upper body move over LF (RF remains in place without wt on it) | 1–& | S |
| Step back in place on RF, shifting entire wt of body over RF | 2–& | S |
| Step on LF near RF | 3 | Q |
| Step in place on RF | & | Q |
| Step in place on LF | 4–& | S |

In shifting the body weight forward or back, there should be a feeling of resistance, similar to that experienced when moving in water.

For the *backward* rock, reverse the above instructions to begin by taking a short step backward on the right foot, shifting the entire upper body weight over that foot.

Have the students repeat the cha-cha basic several times to a verbal count; then they may practice it to a recording that has a well-marked rhythm.

Before permitting the students to take partners, rehearse some of the other easy variations. All figures retain the same rocking characteristic of the cha-cha basic, which stems from shifting the body weight and bending the knees on the first count of each measure.

### The Front Diagonal Crossover

#### The Front Diagonal Crossover

|  | Count | Rhythm |
|---|---|---|
| Step diag fwd toward right on LF | 1–& | S |

| | Count | Rhythm |
|---|---|---|
| Step back in place on RF | 2–& | S |
| Step on LF near RF | 3 | Q |
| Step in place on RF | & | Q |
| Step in place on LF | 4–& | S |

The next measure is the reverse: the dancer steps diagonally across to the left on his right foot on count 1. Repeat the exercise several times.

## The Back Diagonal Crossover

*The Back Diagonal Crossover*

| | Count | Rhythm |
|---|---|---|
| Step diag bkwd to right on LF | 1–& | S |
| Step fwd in place on RF | 2–& | S |
| Step on LF near RF | 3 | Q |
| Step in place on RF | & | Q |
| Step in place on LF | 4–& | S |

The movement is reversed in the second measure by leading backward to the left with the right foot on count 1. Repeat until the exercise is familiar.

## Turns on Slow Counts

Turns are made on the slow counts of the cha-cha basic in challenge position. They may be made in place or traveling slightly. The degree of the turn varies depending on the amount of "push" supplied by the shoulders and upper body. It is important that each step made in turning be of equal duration.

*Turns on Slow Counts*

| | Count | Rhythm |
|---|---|---|
| Step out to side on ball of LF, with toe leading turn to left | 1–& | S |
| Continue turn, stepping across LF to left on RF & changing wt, continuing pivot on ball of RF | 2–& | S |
| Step on LF beside RF | 3 | Q |
| Step in place on RF | & | Q |
| Step in place on LF | 4–& | S |

To reverse directions, the initial step and pivot are done to the right with the right foot. Have the dancers repeat the exercise until it is executed smoothly.

## Turns on Cha, Cha, Cha Counts

Turns are made *in place* on the quick counts.

*Turns on Cha, Cha, Cha Counts*

|  | Count | Rhythm |
|---|---|---|
| Step in place on RF | 1–& | S |
| Step in place on LF | 2–& | S |
| Step to left on LF with toe turned to left | 3 | Q |
| Continue turn bringing RF across LF to left & changing wt to RF | & | Q |
| Step on LF beside RF | 4–& | S |

The dancers reverse the movement by turning to the right on counts 3–&. Have them repeat exercise until the turns are executed smoothly. Initially, the degree of the turn is not important. Eventually, dancers will have the skill and control to make full turns.

## Beginning Sequences with Partners

The cha-cha may be danced in a variety of positions. An easy one for beginning

*Figure 12*

dancers is a variation of the challenge position with the man holding the woman's right hand in his left and her left in his right (see figure 12). Both dancers must keep a slight tension in their arms to assure a strong lead and response. The woman uses the counterpart of the man's steps. He tells her the direction of the movement with his hands as well as his feet.

In the two-hand position, have students practice the cha-cha basic figure until the steps, rhythm, leading and following, and styling are correct and thoroughly understood.

The front diagonal crossover may also be done in the two-hand position. As the man steps diagonally across with his left foot he leads the woman to step across in front of herself with her right foot. Dancers often find it more comfortable to release the hands toward which they are turning. Hands are then quickly rejoined on the cha, cha, cha counts so the dancers are ready to do the figure to the opposite side.

An easy practice sequence is:

2 cha-cha basic figures . . . . . . . . . . . . . . . . . 4 meas

2 front diagonal crossover figures . . . . . . . . . . . . 4 meas

This combination requires changes of direction as well as hand position. Dancers need to be able to move from one figure to another without losing rhythm.

In the same manner, partners may briefly practice the back diagonal crossover. The backward step must be small; an error commonly made by beginners is to step too far away from their partners. The man indicates to his partner that he is going to step back on his left foot by pushing her *right* hand backward, so that she steps backward on her right foot. He then quickly releases her right hand from his left to make the opening more comfortable. The reverse lead is used when beginning with the opposite foot. Hands are rejoined as the dancers return to the face-to-face position.

A simple practice combination may be made using four or six measures each of the cha-cha basic, front diagonal crossover, and back diagonal crossover. The quick changes of direction require concentration but are not difficult.

For the cha-cha figure with turns on slow counts, the dancers may use a completely open challenge position. When that has become comfortable, have them try the turns on cha, cha, cha counts. Dancers' hands and arms move freely as an integral part of the dance; arms and shoulders aid in making the turns.

## The Traveling Cha-Cha Basic

In most cha-cha figures, the cha, cha, cha steps may be made to travel either forward, backward, or sideward. The distance traveled is short, and the footwork remains compact. The technique is the same as that of the two-step in the fox trot (see chapter 5). When the three changes of weight are used in fast dances, the figure is termed a *triplet*.

### The Traveling Cha-Cha Basic

| | Count | Rhythm |
|---|---|---|
| Short rocking step fwd on LF | 1–& | S |
| Step bkwd in place on RF | 2–& | S |
| Short step bkwd on LF | 3 | Q |
| Close RF to LF & change wt | & | Q |
| Short step bkwd on LF | 4–& | S |
| | | |
| Short rocking step bkwd on RF | 1–& | S |
| Step fwd in place on LF | 2–& | S |
| Short step fwd on RF | 3 | Q |
| Close LF to RF & change wt | & | Q |
| Short step fwd on RF | 4–& | S |

After the students practice the traveling sequence with the cha-cha basic, they may apply the same principle to other figures, including those with sideward movements. When they have become thoroughly familiar with all the foregoing figures, permit them to improvise their own sequences using the position that is most comfortable. In figures where hands are joined in some manner, the woman uses the counterpart of the man's steps; in open challenge position, however, each dancer is free to select his own figure (the woman need *not* mirror the man's footwork). Regardless of the position used, the dancers must adhere to the rhythm of the base instruments. In challenge position, dancers move freely around their partners; they are not limited to one set place. The sequence of figures should not be memorized but rather as spontaneous and creative as possible within the limitations of correct styling and rhythm.

As students progress in skill and technique, the next figures may be added to their cha-cha repertoire.

## The Side Break

The side break may be used in either closed or challenge position.

### The Side Break

| | Count | Rhythm |
|---|---|---|
| Step swd to left on LF, with toe pointing fwd (not out), & bend knee slightly; full body wt moves over LF | 1–& | S |
| Step swd to right (in place) on RF, pulling body wt over RF to regain upright position | 2–& | S |
| Step on LF beside RF | 3 | Q |
| Step on RF in place | & | Q |

Step on LF in place                                      · 4 –&        S

The figure is repeated to the right by stepping sideward on the right foot. The sideward step on count 1 should be like a sideward lunge or "fall," with the body weight shifting immediately over the supporting foot. A verbal cue of "Fall, recover, cha, cha, cha" is useful during initial practice of the figure. When dancers take partners, the woman steps to her right as the man steps to his left and vice versa.

## The Chase

The chase is a sequence for fun in which the action says, "You chase me, and I will chase you." While it is an easy figure, beginning dancers are frequently confused by it. The difficulty lies in getting the figure started, because dancers tend to believe they have to begin on a specific foot and turn away from their partners in a specific manner. Like most cha-cha sequences, the chase should be performed freely, starting from any face-to-face position with whichever foot is free on the count of 1.

### The Chase

| Man | Count | Rhythm | Woman |
|---|---|---|---|
| Make a sharp 1/2 turn *away* from your partner, beginning with *either* foot, & turning in *either* direction | 1–& | S | Step in place on free foot |
| Step away from your partner on other foot | 2–& | S | Step in place on other foot |
| Step away from partner | 3 | Q | Step toward partner to "chase" him |
| Close free foot to other foot | & | Q | Close free foot to other foot |
| Step away from partner | 4–& | S | Step toward partner to chase him |

On the next count of 1, *both* dancers make a sharp half-turn to move in the opposite line of direction. The man is then "chasing" the woman. The figure may be repeated until the chasing partner tires of it and does not make the turn away. When the other partner discovers they are both face-to-face again, the chase is over. The dancers then use another cha-cha figure.

## PRACTICE COMBINATIONS

The following exercises give practice in a variety of figures. Any logical hand hold or position may be used, or a variety of holds and positions may be taken in a sequence. Eventually dancers must be encouraged to improvise their own sequences, using varying numbers of measures for each figure.

## Combination 1

4 cha-cha basics . . . . . . . . . . . . . . . . . . . 4 meas
4 front diagonal crossovers . . . . . . . . . . . . . . 4 meas
4 cha-cha basics . . . . . . . . . . . . . . . . . . . 4 meas
4 back diagonal crossovers . . . . . . . . . . . . . . 4 meas
Repeat the sequence until all changes are comfortable.

## Combination 2

4 side breaks . . . . . . . . . . . . . . . . . . . . 4 meas
4 cha-cha basics with turns on slow counts . . . . . . . . . 4 meas
Repeat the sequence until there is no confusion in the change of directions. The dancers' bodies should move freely.

## Combination 3

4 cha-cha basics . . . . . . . . . . . . . . . . . . . 4 meas
1 small CW circle with right hands joined, traveling on
  each of the five changes of wt . . . . . . . . . . . . 6 meas
1 small CCW circle (dancers quickly turn in place to
  join left hands) . . . . . . . . . . . . . . . . . . 6 meas
Repeat the sequence until the transitions and footwork are performed without hesitation.

## Combination 4

4 cha-cha basics . . . . . . . . . . . . . . . . . . . 4 meas
4 cha-cha basics turning on cha, cha, cha counts . . . . . . . 4 meas
4 front diagonal crossovers . . . . . . . . . . . . . . 4 meas
4 side breaks . . . . . . . . . . . . . . . . . . . . 4 meas
Repeat until all changes of body direction are made comfortably and in rhythm.

## Combination 5

Each couple practices the chase sequence using its own choice of number of measures.

# 11

# Rock

Rock 'n' roll music came into being in the early 1950s. It resulted from a combination of rhythm 'n' blues music of the American black culture with the folk song styling of the southern white hill country population—a style once called *hillbilly*. The short musical phrases, with a pulsating two-beat rhythm, produced a repetitive "rocking" sound. A few radio disc jockeys, especially in the New York City area, began to promote "rock 'n' roll" music, a term of their devising, and it quickly gained popularity among teen-age listeners. Because the music was easy to play and used "folk" instruments that were readily available, new rock 'n' roll musical groups mushroomed into being. In the beginning, the star performers were the singers who sang plaintive, folklike lyrics to the music. Later attempts to imitate the big sound of the famous 1940s swing orchestras led young instrumentalists to amplify their music electronically, thus magnifying the natural force of the rhythm.

"Sh-Boom" (1954) and "Rock Around the Clock" (1955) were the first two rock 'n' roll recordings to achieve overwhelming success throughout the United States. Both were in great demand in record shops and tops in popularity on radio stations for weeks.

The new rock music (its shortened name) did not intrude extensively on the ballroom dance scene until 1960 when a young black TV entertainer billed as Chubby Checkers (real name, Ernest Evans, Jr.) introduced a gyrating, twisting, free-style dance he termed the twist. Almost instantly, dancers who had been searching for a dance to fit the new rock rhythm realized that the twist was "it."

It started a revolution, lasting nearly a decade, that virtually replaced older, more traditional forms of ballroom dancing.

Not only were teen-agers attracted to the twist, and the many kindred dances that followed in rapid order, but also older "jet set" members quickly took up the craze. For the more affluent, exclusive dancing clubs were opened. Many used the French term *discotheque* (meaning "a place where records—discs—are kept") in their names, since recorded music was generally played. The terms *discotheque* and *rock* became synonymous with the new type of dancing.

As the rock era progressed, the style of music passed through many phases—"folk rock," "hard rock," "acid rock," "psychedelic rock," and others. By the beginning of the 1970s, the rock *dance* trend had largely subsided, although the music continued to attract vast throngs of young *listeners,* as it originally had in the 1950s. Once again, lyrics have a dominant role in rock music. (For a detailed listing of the major rock dances, see the Chronology of Ballroom Dances at the end of the book.)

## STYLING

Rock 'n' roll dances depart markedly from most of the techniques and positions formerly associated with ballroom dances. The resulting revolution was as radical and controversial as that caused by the waltz and the polka, when they abandoned the strict dance structure dictated by the French court. Ironically, many of the most vocal critics of rock dance were people who had participated in the "jazz" dances of the 1920s, and the swing dances of the 1930s, when those were considered outrageous departures from the accepted standards.

Beginning with the twist, the accepted position for rock dances became the challenge position, or some form of no-contact stance. While this position was not new to ballroom dancing (having been used in balling the jack, the shimmy, the Charleston, the flea hop, the black bottom, bebop, and a number of Latin dances), it had never previously been used in such magnitude. In the majority of rock dances, partners do not attempt to mirror each other's movements; rather each responds to the musical rhythm according to his own desires and ability. Dances frequently developed distinct, characteristic movement patterns and pantomimic gestures, however. For example, the pony consists of prancing leg movements, with head and arms bobbing in rhythm; the monkey depicts the movements of a primate climbing a tree; the skate pantomimes the activity of skating.

Few rock dances follow a definite footwork pattern. All are characterized by vigorous body movements, frequently spontaneous and improvised, that bring forth complicated countermovement patterns. Physical endurance is frequently more important than style.

Rock 'n' roll music is typified by its definitive musical beat. Both foot and body movements may be made on the beat, or the action may be doubled to do two movements to each musical accent.

RHYTHM

Music for rock is composed in 4/4 time, indicating four counts in each measure. Normally, counts 1 and 3 are stressed. The rhythm may be doubled by turning each quarter note into two eighth notes.

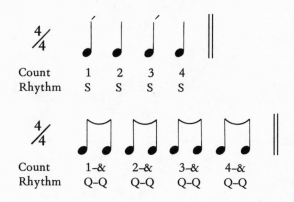

| Count | 1 | 2 | 3 | 4 |
|-------|---|---|---|---|
| Rhythm | S | S | S | S |

| Count | 1–& | 2–& | 3–& | 4–& |
|-------|-----|-----|-----|-----|
| Rhythm | Q–Q | Q–Q | Q–Q | Q–Q |

Individual dancers frequently double their own body and footwork movements in any desired rhythmic sequence.

DANCE MOVEMENTS

Following are typical examples of footwork, knee bends, and body movements of rock dance. The sequences, or any part of them, may be combined in any order to create a free-style rock dance.

Basic Foot Actions

| *Action 1* | *Count* | *Alternative Count* |
|------------|---------|---------------------|
| Step on LF in place | 1 | 1 |
| Bend both knees | 2 | & |
| Step on RF in place | 3 | 2 |
| Bend both knees | 4 | & |

| *Action 2* | | |
|------------|---|---|
| Step on LF in place | 1 | 1 |
| Swing RF fwd | 2 | & |
| Step on RF in place | 3 | 2 |
| Swing LF fwd | 4 | & |

|              *Action 3*              | Count | Alternative Count |
| ------------------------------------ | :---: | :---------------: |
| Step on LF in place                  |   1   |         1         |
| Close RF to LF & change wt           |   2   |         &         |
| Step on LF in place                  |  3–4  |        2–&        |
| Step on RF in place                  |   1   |         3         |
| Close LF to RF & change wt           |   2   |         &         |
| Step on RF in place                  |  3–4  |        4–&        |

|              *Action 4*              | Count | Alternative Count |
| ------------------------------------ | :---: | :---------------: |
| Touch ball of LF to floor            |  1–2  |         1         |
| Step on LF in place                  |  3–4  |         2         |
| Touch ball of RF to floor            |  1–2  |         3         |
| Step on RF in place                  |  3–4  |         4         |

|              *Action 5*              | Count | Alternative Count |
| ------------------------------------ | :---: | :---------------: |
| Step on LF in place                  |   1   |         1         |
| Step on RF in place                  |   2   |         &         |
| Step on LF in place                  |   3   |        2–&        |
| Touch toe of RF to floor             |   4   |    3–&–4–&        |
| Step on RF in place                  |   1   |         1         |
| Step on LF in place                  |   2   |         &         |
| Step on RF in place                  |   3   |        2–&        |
| Touch toe of LF to floor             |   4   |    3–&–4–&        |

|              *Action 6*              | Count |
| ------------------------------------ | :---: |
| Small leap onto LF                   |   1   |
| Close RF to LF (balance) & change wt |   &   |
| Small leap onto LF                   |  2–&  |
| Small leap onto RF                   |   3   |
| Close LF to RF (balance) & change wt |   &   |
| Small leap onto RF                   |  4–&  |

Basic Knee Actions

|              *Action 1*              | Count | Variation |
| ------------------------------------ | :---: | :-------: |
| Bend both knees                      |   1   |     1     |
| Bounce up                            |   &   |     &     |

| | | |
|---|---|---|
| Bend both knees | 2 | 2 |
| Bounce up | & | & |
| Bend both knees | 3 | 3–&–4–& |
| Bounce up | & | |
| Bend both knees | 4 | |
| Bounce up | & | |

| Action 2 | Count | Variation |
|---|---|---|
| Bend both knees | 1 | 1 |
| Bounce up | & | & |
| Bend both knees | 2 | 2 |
| Life one foot on bounce up | & | & |
| Bend both knees | 3 | 3–&–4 |
| Bounce up | & | |
| Bend both knees | 4 | |
| Lift one foot on bounce up | & | |

| Action 3 | Count |
|---|---|
| With wt on LF, bend left knee | 1 |
| Bounce up | & |
| Bend left knee | 2 |
| Bounce up | & |
| Bend left knee | 3 |
| Bounce up | & |
| Bend left knee | 4 |
| Bounce up | & |
| Transfer wt to RF & bend right knee | 1 |
| Bounce up | & |
| Bend right knee | 2 |
| Bounce up | & |
| Bend right knee & bounce up | 3 |
| Bend right knee & bounce up | & |
| Bend right knee & bounce up | 4 |
| Hold | & |

## Basic Hip Actions

Usually hip action in rock dance is a forward, sideward, or backward thrust (bump), or a rotation combining forward, sideward, and backward rolling (grind). A simple example of such a combination follows:

*Basic Hip Action*

|  | Count |
|---|---|
| Thrust right hip diag fwd to right | 1–2 |
| Thrust left hip diag bkwd to left | 3–4 |
| Rotate both hips fwd, swd & bkwd | 1–2–3 |
| Thrust both hips fwd | 4 |

## Basic Actions for Torso, Shoulders, Head, and Arms

The unstructured nature of this kind of dance makes it impossible to classify movements in logical order, but it may be possible to point out some of the more characteristic kinds of body action used.

The *torso* does shakes, jerks, swings, lifts, and drops; the *shoulders* do circles, lifts, drops, jerks, swings, shakes, and flutters; the *head* does shakes, thrusts, jerks, circles, and "pecks;" and the *arms* do whips, jerks, and swings—singly, together, or alternately.

Exploring movement possibilities unlocks a great potential for interaction, alternation, and emphasis on isolated parts of the body.

## PRACTICE COMBINATIONS

Because of the number of parts moving, it is difficult to verbalize all the action in rock dance. The feet move in one pattern for a while and change to something else—at no particular time, just when the dancer decides to change! While the feet are moving, one part, several parts, or the whole body also moves, where, when, and how the individual dancer chooses.

The possible combinations are endless. To structure a specific pattern may be helpful only as an example. Dancers should be encouraged to practice basic steps, watch other rock dancers, and above all try their own sequences and movements.

## Combination 1

| | |
|---|---|
| Basic foot action 1, 4 times . . . . . . . . . . . . . . . . . . | 4 meas |
| Basic hip action, 2 times . . . . . . . . . . . . . . . . . . | 4 meas |
| Foot action 1 & hip action . . . . . . . . . . . . . . . . . . | 4 meas |

8 alternate arm whips . . . . . . . . . . . . . . . . . 2 meas

Foot action 2 with complete head circle, 2 times . . . . . . . . 2 meas

## Combination 2

Foot action 4, with shoulders, head, and arms doing
shakes and jerks for emphasis, 8 times . . . . . . . . . . 16 meas

## Combination 3

Knee action, 2 times . . . . . . . . . . . . . . . . . 4 meas

Knee action 2 with torso and head accents, 2 times . . . . . . 4 meas

Knee action 3 with head and arm accents, 4 times . . . . . . . 8 meas

## Combination 4

Foot action 5, 2 times . . . . . . . . . . . . . . . . 4 meas

Hip and arm thrust accent . . . . . . . . . . . . . . . 2 meas

Knee action 2, 2 times . . . . . . . . . . . . . . . . 4 meas

Hip and arm thrust accent . . . . . . . . . . . . . . . 2 meas

Hip, knee, and head accents . . . . . . . . . . . . . . 4 meas

## SET SEQUENCE DANCES

Not all rock dances are free-style. A few follow a simple set sequence of footwork but each dancer is free to use any appropriate gestures and body rhythm. Dancers frequently accent the rhythm by clapping hands or snapping fingers. Two examples, the Fillmore and the grapevine, are presented.

## The Fillmore

The Fillmore, which originated in San Francisco, is performed by lines of dancers across the dancing area, all facing a common direction. All use the same footwork. It may be danced to any rock music with a well-defined rhythm.

### The Fillmore

|  | Count | Rhythm |
|---|---|---|
| Point RF to right side | 1–& | S |
| Bring RF back beside LF, without changing wt | 2–& | S |
| Point RF to right side | 3–& | S |

*continued*

| | | |
|---|---|---|
| Bring RF back beside LF & change wt to RF | 4-& | S |
| Point LF to left side | 5-& | S |
| Bring LF back beside RF, without changing wt | 6-& | S |
| Point LF to left side | 7-& | S |
| Bring LF back beside RF, *without* changing wt | 8-& | S |
| Short step fwd on LF | 9 | Q |
| Short step fwd on RF, closing RF to LF | & | Q |
| Short step fwd on LF | 10-& | S |
| Short step bkwd on RF | 11 | Q |
| Short step bkwd on LF, closing LF to RF | & | Q |
| Short step bkwd on RF | 12-& | S |
| With wt on both feet, twist feet & body to left, bending knees at same time | 13-& | S |
| With wt on both feet, twist feet & body to face fwd, straightening knees | 14-& | S |
| With wt on both feet, twist feet & body to right, bending knees at same time | 15-& | S |
| With wt on both feet, twist feet & body to face fwd, straightening knees | 16-& | S |

Repeat the sequence until the end of the music.

## The Grapevine

The grapevine derives its name from its crossing and recrossing of the feet at the beginning of the sequence. Dancers stand in lines, facing one another, with the lines close together, but instead of matching two by two, dancers stand to face the *space between* two people in the opposite line; men and women may be mixed in any order. All dancers use identical footwork but may accent body and arm movements in any desired manner. Any well-accented rock music of slow or moderate tempo may be used.

### The Grapevine

| | Count | Rhythm |
|---|---|---|
| Point RF to right side | 1-& | S |
| Step *across* LF to left on RF | 2-& | S |
| Point LF to left side | 3-& | S |
| Step *across* RF to right on LF | 4-& | S |

| | | |
|---|---|---|
| Step bkwd on RF shifting wt bkwd over RF | 5–& | S |
| Step fwd on LF, shifting body to upright position | 6–& | S |
| Step fwd on RF, turning toe to right, making 1/4 turn; dancers from opposite lines begin to change places as they turn | 7 | Q |
| Step on LF, making 1/4 turn to right to complete change of places with opposite line; lines are again facing | & | Q |
| Step in place on RF | 8–& | S |
| Step bkwd on LF shifting wt bkwd over LF | 9–& | S |
| Step fwd on RF, shifting body to upright position | 10–& | S |
| Step in place on LF | 11 | Q |
| Step in place on RF | & | Q |
| Step in place on LF | 12–& | S |

Repeat the sequence to the end of the music.